Illustrations

CW01501766

Figures

IVAN ILLICH FIFTY YEARS LATER

Ivan Illich Fifty Years Later: Situating *Deschooling Society* in His Intellectual and Personal Journey

ROSA BRUNO-JOFRÉ AND
JON IGELMO ZALDÍVAR

UNIVERSITY OF TORONTO PRESS
Toronto Buffalo London

ISBN 978-1-4875-4506-2 (cloth)   ISBN 978-1-4875-4508-6 (EPUB)
ISBN 978-1-4875-4507-9 (PDF)

Library and Archives Canada Cataloguing in Publication
Title: Ivan Illich fifty years later : situating Deschooling society in his intellectual and
  personal journey / Rosa Bruno-Jofré and Jon Igelmo Zaldívar.
Names: Bruno-Jofré, Rosa del Carmen, 1946– author. | Igelmo Zaldívar, Jon,
  1982– author.
Description: Includes bibliographical references and index.
Identifiers: Canadiana (print) 2022019209X | Canadiana (ebook) 20220192154 |
  ISBN 9781487545062 (cloth) | ISBN 9781487545086 (EPUB) |
  ISBN 9781487545079 (PDF)
Subjects: LCSH: Illich, Ivan, 1926–2002. | LCSH: Illich, Ivan, 1926–2002. Deschooling
  society. | LCSH: Educational sociology. | LCSH: Education –
  Philosophy.
Classification: LCC LB885.I442 B78 2022 | DDC 301.01 – dc23

We wish to acknowledge the land on which the University of Toronto Press
operates. This land is the traditional territory of the Wendat, the Anishnaabeg, the
Haudenosaunee, the Métis, and the Mississaugas of the Credit First Nation.

This book has been published with the help of a grant from the Federation for the
Humanities and Social Sciences, through the Awards to Scholarly Publications Program,
using funds provided by the Social Sciences and Humanities Research Council of
Canada.

University of Toronto Press acknowledges the financial support of the Government of
Canada, the Canada Council for the Arts, and the Ontario Arts Council, an agency of
the Government of Ontario, for its publishing activities.

Canada Council   Conseil des Arts
for the Arts   du Canada

ONTARIO ARTS COUNCIL
CONSEIL DES ARTS DE L'ONTARIO
an Ontario government agency
un organisme du gouvernement de l'Ontario

Funded by the   Financé par le
Government   gouvernement
of Canada   du Canada

We dedicate this book to Brenda Reed, Director of the Education Library, Queen's University, for her extraordinary assistance and kindness.

Contents

Acknowledgments

Our gratitude to Brenda Reed, Director of the Queen's University Education Library, and to the staff of Stauffer Library at Queen's. Their cooperation in lending us the volumes of the *CIF Reports* and all the CIDOC publications during the pandemic made this work possible. Our gratitude to Angela Pietrobon, who with eagle eyes checks everything. Our thanks to Megan Patterson, acquisitions editor at University of Toronto Press, who is always attentive to authors' proposals. A big thanks to the blind reviewers. We deeply appreciate the love and support of our families in this enterprise that started with the writing of articles a few years ago and culminated with this book. Our gratitude to Ricardo, Rosa's husband, and Patricia, Jon's wife, and our children.

Foreword

A Brief Trajectory of Ivan Illich

Ivan Illich's intuitive thought appeals to contemporary anarchists and to those looking for ways to remake our humanity, challenge our imprisonment, and transform our existential conditions – from the context of the environment to our health to our use of energy to education. Illich was a sharp critic of modernity and its institutions. Interestingly, he understood modernity as a product of "corrupt" Christianity, and he nourished his initial anti-modernism within the walls of the Pontifical Gregorian University. Thus, his work can be defined as Illichean, yet it is also rooted in his theological background. His turn from a critique of the institutional church to a critique of schooling marks a shift in his intellectual journey. This shift was situated at a particular juncture in his relationship with the Vatican that was signalled by conflict and the death of his protector, the controversial Cardinal Francis Spellman.

On the occasion of the fiftieth anniversary of the publication of Ivan Illich's *Deschooling Society* by Harper & Row, we decided to examine the book with the benefits of temporal distance and a rereading, and in interaction with the author's existential context and experiences – bringing in elements of his biography – as well as theological and philosophical intersections. In this foreword, we attempt to provide the reader unfamiliar with Illich with a biographical frame of reference. Ivan Illich was born in Vienna in 1926 and grew up in a family that embodied the intersection of the old aristocracy (on his father's side) and the new commercial bourgeoisie of Jewish origin. His mother's family was originally Jewish, but they had converted to Catholicism. He died working at his desk in Bremen, Germany, in 2002. He did not have then the attraction and fame that had followed him from the 1960s

Figure F.1. Ivan Illich

to the mid-1970s, although the new century brought a return to Illich's writings as well as memories of his charismatic presence.

Illich left Austria in 1942 with his mother and siblings after the death of his father, when the family lost the category of half-Aryan to be labelled half-Jew.[1] In Rome in 1944, he started studies at the Pontifical

---

1 See details in chapter 1.

Gregorian University, immersed in what he recalled as obscurantist theology, and where he also completed his master's degree in theology and philosophy; in 1951, he graduated from the University of Salzburg, Austria, with a doctoral degree and was ordained as a priest in Rome.[2] He was a travelling student and priest in the making.

That same year, he left the Vatican and the promise of a diplomatic career to move to the Archdiocese of New York. There he was welcomed by the conservative and controversial Cardinal Francis Spellman. After ministering to newly arrived Puerto Ricans in New York, Illich went to Puerto Rico after being appointed as vice-rector of the Catholic University of Ponce. He stayed from 1956 to 1960. It was there that he met Everett Reimer, who would introduce him to educational issues.[3]

In 1960, he returned to New York, after adventurous travels in Latin America. Illich then became involved in the project to train missionaries for a program known as the Papal Volunteers for Latin America (1960) and in supporting John XXIII's appeal to religious congregations to send missionaries to Latin America (1961). Thus emerged, with Illich as its executive director, the Centre for Intercultural Formation (CIF), housed at Fordham University, New York. He then opened a network of centres in Cuernavaca in 1961, in the Hotel Chulavista, Mexico. Missionaries went to the Centro de Investigaciones Culturales (Cultural Research Center) (CIC), a residence for missionaries where they also learned Spanish.[4]

We describe Cuernavaca as a refractory micro-cosmos, as it was the right setting for Illich's prophetic insights. There he was close to Bishop Sergio Méndez Arceo, social psychoanalyst Erich Fromm, and Prior of the Benedictine Convent Gregorio Lemercier in an environment of experimentation and *aggiornamento*, even before Vatican II. Psychoanalysis was in the air. Illich inserted himself in the church's project to modernize Latin America in line with the US Alliance for Progress's mission to stop "communism" and the expansion of Protestantism; the centres were financed by the Latin American Bureau of the National Catholic Welfare Council, of which Maryknoll John Considine, a promotor of the papal programs, was the director. The Bureau provided

---

2 Todd Hartch, *The Prophet of Cuernavaca: Ivan Illich and the Crisis of the West* (Oxford: Oxford University Press, 2015), 4–6.

3 See details in chapter 1.

4 Rosa Bruno-Jofré and Jon Igelmo Zaldívar, "The Center for Intercultural Formation, Cuernavaca, Mexico, Its Reports (1962–1967) and Illich's Critical Understanding of Mission in Latin America," *Hispania Sacra* LXVI (July–December 2014): 457–587. See also chapter 2.

Illich with $75,000 to initiate the creation of the centres. The counterpart of Cuernavaca was placed in 1961 in Brazil, opening first in Anápolis and then moving to Petrópolis in 1962.

Illich worked out from the beginning a counterapproach, often qualified as subversive, for a resignification of the role of the missionary. By 1964, Illich had worked out the first move to break with his sponsors, by taking control of the publications for missionaries, and in 1966 he moved the Centro Intercultural de Documentación (Intercultural Documentation Center) (CIDOC) that had been inside CIC to Chulavista, separating it from the church. It became an intellectual and political hub at which major leaders and authors of the time converged, including Paulo Freire, Paul Goodman, Jonathan Kozol, Peter Berger, and Augusto Salazar Bondy, among many others. Illich closed CIDOC in 1976, after which he was not engaged in dialogue with the "big people of the world."[5]

Illich went through a process of radicalization clearly conveyed in his critical writings of the church as an institution, namely, its bureaucracy, its political role in Latin America, the seminaries, and the role of the priests. Thus, "The Seamy Side of Charity" (1967), with its anti-imperialist tone, and "The Vanishing Clergyman" (1967), with its critique of celibacy, attracted attention in major publications in the United States, Mexico, and Europe in the late 1960s. Particularly appealing were his critical stands about the church as institution, as it – in opposition to the church as She, referring to the traditions and spirituality. Then, his conflict with the Vatican in 1968 was widely publicized. At that time, he had lost the protection of Spellman, who had died in December 1967.

Illich moved from a critique of the church to a critique of schooling as an institution of modernity, but he built analogies to the church as an institution. He produced three texts about schooling before the precursors of *Deschooling Society*, published by Harper & Row in 1971, with most of its chapters having been published in *CIDOC Cuadernos*, as will be discussed in chapter 4.[6]

---

5 Valentina Borremans and Jean Robert, "Prefacio" [Preface], in *Ivan Illich: Obras completas reunidas*, vol. 1 [Ivan Illich: Collected Works, vol. 1] (Mexico: Fondo de Cultura Económica, 2006), 14.

6 Ivan Illich, "La escuela, esa vieja y gorda vaca sagrada: en América Latina abre un abismo de clases y prepara a una elite y con ella el fascismo" [The School, that Old and Fat Sacred Cow: In Latin America it Opens an Abyss between Classes and Prepares an Elite and with Her, Fascism], Mexico, D. F., 78 (789), 7 August 1968; Ivan Illich, "La metamorphosis de la escuela: Mensaje en ocasión de la graduación celebrada en el recinto Universitario de Río Piedras, Puerto Rico," *El Día*, reprinted in CIDOC Cuernavaca, *CIDOC Cuaderno* no. 44: 148/55; Ivan Illich,

The book was well received in the early 1970s. There had been other successful books critiquing schooling, in particular those written by Paul Goodman and Jonathan Kozol and the studies of social historians.[7] However, *Deschooling Society*, in its apocalyptic tone, announced Illich's view that the end of the era of scholarization had been reached. It was a time of uncertainty and crisis in which the Yom Kippur War in October 1973 had led to the realization of the dependency on oil and to economic uncertainty. In 1972, the impact of *The Limits to Growth*, commissioned by the Club of Rome, reporting on economic and population growth with a finite supply of resources and the limits of the system, substantiated the idea of change.[8] We needed alternative models on both sides of the Iron Curtain. It was a time when decolonization and its impact on life and intellectual discourses opened up new questions about education as an intervening tool. The processes of the Latin American countries had been involved in different attempts at social transformation in the 1960s and early 1970s, including looking at education in new, transformative ways. Paulo Freire's pedagogy was an example of an epistemological rupture in the way to approach adult education and social change.

Other publications of Illich's in the 1970s attracted attention, for example, *Celebration of Awareness* (Anchor Books, 1971), *Tools for Conviviality* (Harper & Row, 1973), *Energy and Equity* (Marion Boyars, 1974), and *Medical Némesis* (Calder and Boyars, 1975). We would note, for example, that the author of Illich's obituary published by *The Lancet* wrote that *Medical Némesis* had "something of a prophetic quality."[9] However, the successful reception of *Deschooling Society* did not last very long.

Illich's ideas of the disestablishment of schooling from the state and his questioning of schooling having the monopoly of education as

---

"The Futility of Schooling in Latin America," *Saturday Review*, 20 April 1968, 57–9 and 74–5.

7 Paul Goodman, *Growing Up Absurd: Problems of Youth in the Organized Society* (New York: Random House, Vintage Books, 1960); Michael Katz, *The Irony of Early School Reform: Educational Innovation in Mid-nineteenth Century Massachusetts* (New York: Teachers College Press, 2001; first published in 1968); Jonathan Kozol, *Death at an Early Age: The Destruction of the Hearts and Minds of Negro Children in the Boston Public Schools* (New York: Bantam Books, 1967).

8 Donella H. Meadows, Dennis L. Meadows, Jorgen Randers, and William W. Behrens, *The Limits to Growth* (New York: Potomac Associates – Universe Books, 1972).

9 Pearce Wright, "Obituary. Ivan Illich," *The Lancet* 361, no. 9352 (11 January 2003): 185. https://www.thelancet.com/journals/lancet/article/PIIS0140-6736(03)12233-7/fulltext.

expounded in *Deschooling Society* played a marginal role in the educative debate of the 1980s. Illich himself, as we indicate in chapter 4, became critical of his own approach. The political context of the 1980s was characterized by strong neoliberal policies (sponsored by Margaret Thatcher, Ronald Reagan, and Helmut Kohl). It was a time of repression of social and cultural movements, a time of counter-revolutionary wars in Central America sponsored by the United States, and the end of the decade witnessed the disintegration of the Soviet Bloc. The shift was dramatic, and critical thinking in education had difficulties in gaining strength and reaccommodating this shift.

Meanwhile, new paradigms along with new epistemologies and theories emerged, inspired by the linguistic turn, cultural history, epistemologies, including feminist epistemologies, and post-colonial theories nourished by the social movements of the 1960s and early 1970s and the processes of decolonization. The influence of Foucault in the intellectual world was felt, particularly his understanding of power and its capillary workings in spheres of culture, ideas, and everyday practices.[10] At the end of the 1970s, Illich was engaged in a new search. In 1982, he shared the draft of *Gender*, in which he explored the transition from the proportionality of gender to the world of economic sex, at the University of California at Berkeley.[11] The reaction from feminist scholars was strong. One of the co-authors of this book remembers how much *Gender* actually upset her. After the controversy, Illich stopped being a fashionable author, and he moved in new directions. His work then was led by a preoccupation with the transition from a textual to a cybernetic image of the self[12] and to the relation of present and past, an example being *H2O and the Waters of Forgetfulness* (1985) and the lectures he delivered in the 1980s and 1990s.[13] Illich examined the certainties of modernity and how those certainties were given credibility in many presentations and articles. Of interest here is his book with Barry Sanders, *ABC: The Alphabetization of the Popular Mind*.[14] Often, his claims had a radical and absolute tone. In the second half of the 1980s and in the 1990s, he returned to education with a critical view of what he had expounded in *Deschooling Society*, moving to explore the

10 Daniel T. Rodgers, *Age of Fracture* (Cambridge, MA: Belknap Press of Harvard University, 2011), 107.

11 Ivan Illich, *Gender* (New York: Marion Boyars, 1983).

12 David Cayley, *Ivan Illich in Conversation* (Toronto: House of Anansi Press, 1992), 37.

13 Ivan Illich, *H2O and the Waters of Forgetfulness: Reflections on the Historicity of Stuff* (Dallas: Dallas Institute of Humanities and Culture, 1985).

14 Ivan Illich and Barry Sanders, *ABC: The Alphabetization of the Popular Mind* (New York: Marion Boyars, 1988).

Figure F.2. *mind on horizon*, digital photograph, by Alan Wilkinson, 2010.

This image documents a moment on a seemingly isolated electronic billboard located on the roof of a building near Times Square in New York City. In various studies of the "mind" one attribute that is commonly addressed, but seldom settled upon, is the connection of this term to a wide variety of human realities, such as imagination, memory, the brain, the body, cognition, morality, and emotion. This visual isolation of "Mind…" upon an urban horizon may prompt individual reflection.

circumstances leading to the rise of the idea of and discourse behind educational needs. One can do a postmodern reading of Illich, as some of his ideas were not far from Foucault; at the same time, we can do a Catholic non-magisterial reading.[15]

---

15 Rosa Bruno-Jofré and Jon Igelmo Zaldívar, "Ivan Illich's Late Critique of *Deschooling Society*: "I Was Largely Barking Up the Wrong Tree," *Educational Theory* 62, no. 5 (2012): 573–89.

In the last few decades leading up to the fiftieth anniversary of *Deschooling Society*, there has been some inspiring intellectual production centred on the work and thought of Ivan Illich. This development has come along with a renewed interest in his thinking. A new generation of readers has approached Illich's work in search of alternative pedagogies, particularly in light of new technologies. These are readers who are removed by one or two generations from the events that characterized the 1960s and early 1970s. Instead, these readers have had as points of reference a different constellation of events, such as the Zapatista Indigenous movement in Mexico in 1994, the demonstrations in Seattle in 1999, the digital context, the ecological crisis, the attack of 9/11 in 2001, the US war in Iraq, the financial crisis of 2008, the Arab Spring, and citizen mobilizations, such as Occupy Wall Street in the United States and 15 M in Spain. Moreover, the current context in 2022 generates a new reading. It is a crowded context in which we can identify the emergence of the power of the right and of supremacist groups, as well as anti-racist movements, Indigenous movements and claims, human rights advocacy, a focus on gender- and sex-inclusive issues, and women's voices denouncing sexual harassment. We also cannot neglect to mention the pandemic and the obvious climate crisis, in addition to social and economic inequalities accentuated by neoliberal policies. The reception of Illich's writings and his readings are obviously permeated with the contextual and configurational lenses.

Ivan Illich was a sophisticated thinker with a profound understanding of Western history and philosophy, and above all a Catholic thinker who, by and large, wrote from a theological perspective. We have traced in *Deschooling Society* various ideas of the complex constellation that framed his Illichean critique of modern institutions and processes of institutionalization, including his early neo-scholastic and anti-modern foundation, his discovery of St. Thomas through Jacques Maritain, and his constant search for new ways of knowing. It has been a journey that has moved us to think across Western temporalities. We invite you, the reader, to enter into Illich's labyrinth of thought.

IVAN ILLICH FIFTY YEARS LATER

Introduction

Over the last few years, we have worked with various dimensions of Ivan Illich's thinking with particular reference to his work in Cuernavaca. In this book, we focus on *Deschooling Society* on occasion of the fiftieth anniversary of its first publication in 1970 with the title *The Dawn of Epimethean Man and Other Essays*, and as *Deschooling Society* by Harper & Row in 1971.[1] A central question guiding our interest and research was: how did Illich reach the point of writing *Deschooling Society*?[2] To answer, we went to the theological roots of his thought as well as to the various intellectual and ideological strands that would contribute to his own constellation of ideas.

Illich produced an Illichean critique of schooling that can be defined by its eclecticism. The book, a plea to liberate education from schooling and separate schooling from the state, kept elements of his early theological formation at Pontifical Gregorian University; it also shows his urge to go back to pre-modern Christianity, and his familiarity with – but not embracement of – the emergence of "nouvelle théologie" in Europe as well as with phenomenology and personalism. Illich's work reflected the influence of Jacques Maritain. In fact, Maritain was instrumental in generating Illich's lifelong interest in Thomas Aquinas, and Illich

---

1 Ivan Illich, *The Dawn of Epimethean Man and Other Essays* (CIDOC Cuaderno no. 54, 1970); Ivan Illich, *Deschooling Society* (New York: Harper & Row, 1971). Harper & Row selected the title, not Illich.
2 We consulted the documentation from the Intercultural Centre for Documentation (CIDOC) placed in 1976 at the Daniel Cosío Villegas Library, El Colegio de México, Mexico DF, as well as the complete collection of the *CIF Reports: Cultures, The Church, The Americas,* compiled in six volumes and published by CIDOC, and the various other series also published by CIDOC. We also consulted extensive secondary sources.

embraced Maritain's notion of an emancipatory engagement with the secular world. Once in New York, exercising his role as pastor, he was part of the circle involved with *Commonweal Magazine*, a magazine critical of orthodox positions and in which Jacques Maritain, Dorothy Day, Thomas Merton, and Hannah Arendt had published. Illich's experience in Puerto Rico defined his thinking and praxis on education and schooling, as it was there that he met Everett Reimer and Leopold Kohr. The influence of the circle in Cuernavaca – with Bishop Sergio Méndez Arceo, Erich Fromm, and Gregorio Lemercier – and the evolution of the centres Illich ran there put him in touch with psychoanalysis, liberation theology, and anti-imperialist views. Illich would not particularly subscribe to any of those positions. We have identified in his eclecticism an axial line guiding his analysis.

This guiding line in Illich's critique of schooling was the persistence of his Catholic view, albeit iconoclastic, being grounded in a critique of the church as institution and of the corruption of the Christian message by modernity. This Catholic view was intertwined – not necessarily articulated – with secular currents of thought. His Thomistic framework and theological thinking is fundamental to understanding his concern with schooling as an imposed necessity, his search for freedom of will, and his view of the self as agent. His language was also inspired by Belgium Jesuit Émile Mersch's vision that the life of Jesus on earth prolongs in the church, as they are not separate lives. Mersch wrote that "the historical Christ is the same as the mystical Christ; his historical life was already his mystical life."[3] Thomism along with Illich's theological background, may have led to the overall universal understandings of issues of inequality in education reflected in *Deschooling Society*, although the book neglected to discuss the major social movements of the time, including Indigenous issues in Latin America. The roots of Illich's anti-state, anti-modernist line of thought can be traced to his formative years and the church's long critique of modernity and of the state; they contain elements from the Catholic anti-modernist view that society as a whole had to be infused with Catholic values, the old *ethos* of the church. In other words, this was a third way, neither medievalist – a restorative current after the First World War – nor modernist, but often called ultra-modern (beyond modernity).

We have identified some existential turning points that influenced Illich's public life and intellectual direction in moving from a critique

---

3 Émile Mersch, S.J., "La vide historique de Jésus et sa vie mystique," *Nouvelle Revue Théologique* 60, no. 1 (January 1933): 5–20.

of the church to a critique of schooling. An important one was the protection Illich had from the controversial right-wing Cardinal Francis Spellman (known for his predatory sexual behaviour), from the time Illich moved from Rome to New York until Spellman's death in 1967. Another key turning point was his relationship with Everett Reimer and his familiarization with educational matters in Puerto Rico. Particularly powerful was Illich's own insertion within the configuration of forces and ideas that embodied the institutional response of the Catholic Church, in alliance with US policies, to social unrest in Latin America. This led to the creation of the centres in Mexico (Cuernavaca, 1961) and Brazil (Anápolis, moved to Petrópolis in 1962), where he worked with Archbishop Hélder Pessoa Câmara. The centres prepared missionaries (following John XXIII's call in 1961) and papal volunteers following Illich's contestarian vision of the role of the missionary and not the dictates from the Vatican. Another key point was his decision to take control of the centres' reports, known as the *CIF Reports*, in 1964. The creation of the Centre for Intercultural Documentation (CIDOC) in 1963 represented a move signalling a search for independence from the US church, which financially supported the centres. When CIDOC was moved to Rancho Tetela from Chulavista, where it resided within the Centre for Intercultural Research/CIC (the centre that received missionaries to Latin America), to become an independent intellectual hub in 1966, Illich ended the relationship with the Latin American Bureau of the National Catholic Welfare Conference and also with John Considine and members of the US Catholic hierarchy.[4] His critique of the institutionalized church and of the church's participation in US interventions in social projects in Latin America (the Alliance for Progress was a major macro-frame), clearly expressed in "The Seamy Side of Charity" and "The Vanishing Clergyman," led to Illich's consequent conflict with the Vatican in 1968.[5] Illich had lost Spellman's protection – when he died in December 1967 – and moved away from a critique of the church to engage in a critique of schooling as an institution of modernity.

There was a transition to *Deschooling Society* starting in 1968, with three texts published after Spellman's death: "The Futility of Schooling in Latin America," questioning the school as a model based on

---

4 See chapter 2, in particular on the centres and their programs.
5 Ivan Illich, "The Seamy Side of Charity," in *Celebration of Awareness: A Call of Institutional Revolution* (New York: Anchor Books, 1971), 57–84; Ivan Illich, "The Vanishing Clergyman," in *Celebration of Awareness: A Call of Institutional Revolution* (New York: Anchor Books, 1971), 39–56.

meritocracy moving towards progress;[6] "The School, That Old and Fat Sacred Cow: In Latin America It Opens an Abyss between Classes and Prepares an Elite and with Her, Fascism," published in August 1968 in the Mexican magazine *Siempre*, questioning the notion of the school as a panacea for social integration;[7] and "The School's Metamorphosis" ("La metamorphosis de la escuela"), in which he denounces the unfairness of the system.[8] During the conflict with the Vatican, he stated his faithfulness to the church (as It, the institution) and the doctrine of the magisterium and insisted that his intention was not to destroy the church even as an institution. He did not engage in a theological understanding of social justice or of what he thought was the specific function of the church, "the annunciation of the Gospel."[9]

Deschooling Society is placed in time in the "long 1960s" – late 1950s to mid-1970s – a time that signalled a shift to social transformation and new conceptions of education within a broad spectrum – from cognitive psychology to Freire's literacy method and related challenging ways of thinking about democratic pedagogies, which emerged from revolutionary discourses and practices in Latin America. The Vatican II Council generated a paradigmatic shift aiming at an *aggiornamento* of the church doctrines with modernity. Within this overall framework, we consider Illich's own intellectual background and experiential acumen; his positioning regarding the institutional church and the enactment of his view of the church as a spiritual force affecting societal changes – explaining why he did not embrace liberation theology; and the critique of modernity from a Catholic standpoint that reveals various layers of temporality in his argument, including early Christianity and medieval times. It is not new to say that *Deschooling Society* is an apophatic analysis. The topic he discussed in the book is not new. Paul Goodman, Kozol, and John Holt had written harsh critiques of

---

6 Ivan Illich, "The Futility of Schooling in Latin America," *Saturday Review*, 20 April 1968, 57–9 and 74–5, particularly 74–5; reprinted in *CIDOC Cuaderno*, no. 20 (Cuernavaca, Mexico: CIDOC, 1968), 66/1–66/10.

7 Ivan Illich, "La escuela, esa vieja y gorda vaca sagrada; en América Latina abre un abismo de clases y prepara a una elite y con ella el fascismo" (Cuernavaca, Mexico: CIDOC, 1968), 68/95. Originally published in *Siempre Mexico*, D.F., 78 (789), 7 August 1968. Translation by the authors.

8 Ivan Illich, "La metamorphosis de la escuela: mensaje en ocasión de la graduación celebrada en el recinto, Universitario de Río Piedras, Puerto Rico," *El Día*, Mexico, 2 July 1969, 10; reprinted in *CIDOC Cuaderno*, no. 44 (Cuernavaca, Mexico: CIDOC, November 1969), 148/55.

9 Ivan Illich, "The Powerless Church," in Ivan Illich, *Celebration of Awareness: A Call for Institutional Revolution* (New York: Doubleday, 1971), 87–94, quotation on 87.

schooling. Everett Reimer's book *School is Dead* (1971) shares similarities with Illich's *Deschooling Society*, in that Reimer opposed compulsory schooling and wished to free education from schooling.[10] Illich and Reimer were engaged in joint research and in the end decided to follow separate ways. What is original then about *Deschooling Society*? Illich brought a theological dimension to the analysis while placing the critique as a critique of modernity and the idea of progress, went back to the Thomist idea of agency, and questioned the institutionalization of values. He did not engage with a political project or vision.

Deschooling Society contains statements/theses, such as equal educational opportunity is desirable, but to equate this with obligatory schooling is to confuse salvation with the church (an analogy with the church); schooling has become an imposed necessity (following Thomas Aquinas, natural necessity is not repugnant to the will); and not only education but social reality itself has become schooled. His alternative is based on the idea that people acquire most knowledge from outside the school, the school being by and large a place of confinement.[11] He wanted there to be a sense of personal responsibility when teaching and learning (a theological search for freedom, freedom of the will, the self as agent, and a Thomistic concern with imposed necessity) – a transformation of consciousness in relation to the nature of learning that does not conceive learning as merchandise or as an institutional goal. He wanted to liberate learning in the same way he wanted to liberate the relationship with God, creating learning as a search for freedom in God. The dawn of Epimetheus is particularly explored in spite of its apparent disconnection to the rest of the book since it embodied his conception of the modern human and questioned the replacement of values dear to traditional Catholicism – such as hope, faith, and love being replaced with expectation, planning, and charity.

Illich's arguments supporting his positioning are that the school has become the world religion of a modernized proletariat making futile promises of salvation; thus, both rich and poor depend on schools and hospitals to guide their lives and define for them what is legitimate and what is not; and schools discourage and disable the poor from taking control of their learning. He argued that no matter how rich a country is, it cannot afford a school system that can meet the demands that the systems itself creates. Obligatory schooling polarizes society, reproducing inequality, and countries are rated, he said, like castes.[12]

---

10 Everett Reimer, *School is Dead* (New York: Doubleday & Co. 1971).
11 Illich, *Deschooling Society*, 10. For this part, see chapter 4.
12 Illich, *Deschooling Society*, chapter 1.

Figure I.1. Dalmatian Coast, Croatia.

Source: Licensed under the Creative Commons Attribution – Share Alike 2.0 (https://
creativecommons.org/licenses/by-sa/2.0/deed.en), via Wikimedia Commons, available
at https://commons.wikimedia.org/wiki/File:Dalmatia_coast.jpg. Photograph by
Markus Bernet, 26 July 2005.

He made the case that learning has become a kind of merchandise
or institutional goal; the criteria for evaluation used in schools and
the curriculum, with the latter broken up into prefabricated blocks, is
based on the myth of measurement; and the idea of self-perpetuating
progress is also a myth on which the school is based.[13] Illich's solution was to disestablish schools, meaning moving them away from the
state, with his most controversial statement being that funds should be
channeled to the beneficiary, mentioning Milton Friedman's system of
tuition grants.[14] He proposed the use of educational webs as a possible

---

13 Illich, *Deschooling Society*, chapter 3.
14 Illich, *Deschooling Society*, 6. Illich wrote, "Funds would be channeled to the
    beneficiary enabling him to buy his share of the schooling of his choice. If such
    credit were limited to purchases which fit into a school curriculum, it would tend to

alternative within the context of an emerging counterculture and self-motivated learning. The separation of schooling from the state would have, in his view, the revolutionary potential to destroy the social order.

Illich's own critique of his positioning in *Deschooling Society*, written particularly in the 1990s, makes him worthwhile to study as an intellectual figure able to reframe his criticism of schooling and education in light of what he saw as his mistake. He used the well-known phrase "I was largely barking up the wrong tree" to refer to his "mistake." He wrote, "Much more important than the disestablishment of schools, I began to see, was the reversal of those trends that make of education a pressing need rather than a gift of gratuitous leisure."[15] In closing the analysis of *Deschooling Society* in this book, we cite Illich's words from his later years: "If people are seriously to think about deschooling their life, and not just escape from the corrosive effects of compulsory schooling, they could do no better than to develop the habit of setting a mental question mark beside all discourse on young people's 'educational needs' or 'learning needs,' or about their need for a 'preparation for life.' I would like them to reflect on the historicity of these very ideas. Such reflection would take the new crop of deschoolers a step further from where the younger and somewhat naïve Ivan was situated, back when talk of 'deschooling' was born."[16]

---

provide greater equality of treatment, but would not thereby increase the equality of social claims."

15 Ivan Illich, foreword to *Deschooling Our Lives*, ed. Matt Hern (Philadelphia: New Society Publishers, 1996), viii.

16 Illich, foreword to *Deschooling Our Lives*, x.

1 Ivan Illich: From the Dalmatian Coast, through Vienna, to Rome (1926–1951)

Going to the Roots

This narrative seeks to explore the formative years of Ivan Illich Regenstreif-Ortlieb (his last name was spelled Illiç in Croatian), and to search for early intellectual connections that informed his thinking and the sources of those connections. In the last instance, we explore his choices in light of new contexts that may or may not have defined his formation. In particular, we attempt to explain the hybrid patterns of his thought evident in *Deschooling Society*. An important question that we start with is how did he reach the point of publishing *Deschooling Society* with Harper & Row? Illich published this impactful book after only three years of publishing controversial articles on education.

Ivan Illich was born in Vienna in 1926 and spent part of his early years on Brac Island, located on the Dalmatian coast of the Adriatic Sea. Illich himself spoke about his early visit to the island in a conference held in Tokyo on 21 March 1982, to which he was invited as a keynote speaker:

> This man who speaks to you was born 55 years ago in Vienna. One month after his birth he was put on a train, and then on a ship and brought to the Island of Brac. Here, in a village on the Dalmatian coast, his grandfather wanted to bless him. My grandfather lived in the house in which his family has lived since the time when Muromachi ruled in Kyoto. Since then on the Dalmatian Coast many rulers have come and gone – the doges of Venice, the sultans of Istanbul, the corsairs of Almissa, the emperors of Austria, and the kings of Yugoslavia. But the many changes in the uniform and language of the governors had altered little in daily life during those 500 years. The very same olive-wood rafters still supported the roof of my grandfather's house. Water was still gathered from the same stone slabs

on the roof. The wine was pressed in the same vats, the fish caught from the same kind of boat, and the oil came from trees planted when Edo was in its youth.

My grandfather had received news twice a month. The news now arrived by steamer in three days; formerly, by boat, it had taken five days to arrive. When I was born, for the people who lived off the main routes, history still flowed slowly, imperceptibly. Most of the environment was in the commons. People lived in houses they had built; moved on streets that had been trampled by the feet of their animals; were autonomous in the procurement and disposal of their water; could depend on their own voices when they wanted to speak up. All this changed with my arrival in Brac.[1]

A new unstable historical reality had emerged by the end of the war. Four empires had collapsed: the Austro-Hungarian, the Ottoman, the Russian, and the German. The map was redrawn not only in Europe but also in Africa, Asia, and the Middle East. Colonialism continued, and Great Britain and France were the major colonial powers.[2] Illich's younger years were framed by the 1930s scenario: the emergence of Nazism and fascism, and the civil war in Spain (1936–9) that ended with the instauration of Franco's regime, which brought Catholic integrism to Spain, referring to the alliance of church and state and a Catholic Church that reconquered the state. The 1930s was a decade of aggressions that marked the path to the Second World War, including the German invasion of Austria in 1938, a time when Illich went to school in Vienna.[3] All of these events, along with his family background, became powerful intersections in his young life.

His family background was complex. Illich's father, Gian Pietro Ilič, was an aristocratic Croatian, a practising Catholic, an engineer, and a wealthy landowner, while his mother was from a Sephardic Jewish family that had converted to Catholicism.[4] It is said that he

---

1 Ivan Illich, *In the Mirror of the Past: Lectures and Address, 1978–1990* (New York: Marion Boyars, 1992), 52.

2 Eric Hobsbawm, *The Age of Extremes: The Short Twentieth Century* (London: Abacus, 1996), 7.

3 Hobsbawm, *The Age of Extremes*, 37. Among these aggressions were the Japanese invasion of Manchuria in 1931, the Italian invasion of Ethiopia in 1935, the German and Italian intervention in the Spanish Civil War (1936–9), the German invasion of Austria in 1938, the German occupation of Czechoslovakia (1938–9), the Italian occupation of Albania in 1939, and the German occupation of Poland in 1939.

4 Ivan Illich's father was Gian Pietro (Piero) Ilić (1890–1942). His paternal grandparents were Gian Domenico Ilić (1858–1934) and Olga Ilić (Katalinić) (1870–1960). His

learned many of the languages he mastered at the knees of governesses.[5] His maternal grandfather was Fritz Regenstreif, a well-known businessman in the wood industry who owned a sawmill in Bosnia. The material expression of their comfortable socio-economic situation was the family's country house in Vienna, known as Villa Regenstreif.[6]

In the interview with David Cayley published with the title *Ivan Illich in Conversation*, Illich added that after his birth, "at the age of three months, I was exported, with my nurse, to Dalmatia to be shown to my grandfather and to be baptized, there, in Split, on Vidovdan, the Day of Great Liberation, the first of December. There I grew up, spending a part of the year in Dalmatia, a part with the other grandparent in Vienna, and a part of the year in France or wherever my parents were."[7] His own social background embodied modern society, in particular the intersection of the old aristocracy with the new commercial bourgeoisie of Jewish origin.

The house in Vienna where Illich was raised together with his twin brothers, Villa Regenstreif, was one of the most stately houses representing the power of the Viennese bourgeoisie. Surrounded by lakes and gardens, it was a sumptuous house on the outskirts of Vienna on Pötzleinsdorfer Straße. It was built between 1913 and 1917 by architect Friedrich Ohman, who combined romantic and baroque styles in the design. The house had many private rooms and an open salon, and a movie room, bowling alley, and greenhouse in the basement.[8] The rich grandfather was able to protect his family from the Gestapo. The policemen visited them weekly. It was a traumatic experience for the family, who flew to Italy when the grandfather died.[9]

Illich's social background, related savoir faire, and family connections, which extended to even the United States, set the stage for his movements across the world. His mother, Ellen Rose, had intellectual

---

mother's name was Ellen Rose Illich (Regenstreif Ortlieb) (1901–65), and she was called Maexie by the family. His maternal grandparents were Fritz (Pucki) Regenstreif (1866–1941) and Johanna Regenstreif (Ortlieb) (1877–1934).

5 Francine du Plessix Gray, *Divine Disobedience: Profiles in Catholic Radicalism* (New York: Alfred A. Knopf, 1970), 242.

6 Illich, *In the Mirror of the Past*, 52.

7 David Cayley, "An Interview with Ivan Illich by David Cayley," edited by Chris Mercogliano, *SKOLE: The Journal of Alternative Education* 14, no. 1 (1997): 168–81, quotation on 171.

8 See "Let's Keep It," Burgl Czeitschner Film Production, 2021, https://letskeepit.at /de_regenstreif-illich.htm.

9 See "Let's Keep It," 2021.

and artistic contacts, and she was the one who introduced her son to poets and to French Catholic theologian Jacques Maritain, who would have a great influence on Illich. This was a key encounter for tracing one of Illich's connections to his anti-modernist, anti-state line of thought. In fact, Maritain would become the representative of a relativized Thomism capable of integrating with contemporary culture.[10] Moreover, Maritain in his early days was familiar with anti-modernist forms of politics, mainly neo-medievalism and the emergence of a current referred to as ultra-modernist (beyond modernity) and held points in common with the Catholic medievalism of the 1920s. He agreed with Georg Moenious that "Catholicism could not sequester itself into the private sphere, and that society as a whole had to be suffused with Catholic values"[11] and that "a natural political order would be deeply federal and pluralistic, respecting natural hierarchies and local power structures instead of sucking them into the maw of a centralizing state."[12] Catholic medievalism, as Chapel said, provided tools for a critique of capitalism and of the secular state.[13] This is a point we will explore further in relation to *Deschooling Society*.

Illich stated to Cayley that he was brought up without much schooling. When he was six and his normal languages were French, Italian, and German, he said, his mother wanted to put him in a school in Vienna, but the required testing process resulted in him being considered "retarded." He then spent two years in his grandmother's library.[14] Of his education, he noted, "Yes, I went to school, but only by bits."[15] Illich lived in Vienna in Villa Regenstreif until his grandfather died in 1941. In spite of the earlier test result, he went on to pursue high degrees in distinguished educational institutions. Between the time he was ten (1936) and fifteen years of age, he was a student at the prestigious Piaristengymnasium in Vienna. After his father died in 1942, the family lost their former category of half-Aryan to be labelled half-Jew. Illich, his mother, and his two twin brothers moved to Florence, Italy, after his father's death, where he completed his high

10 Jürgen Mettepenningen, *Nouvelle théologie/New Theology: Inheritor of Modernism, Precursos of Vatican II* (New York: T & T Clark International, 2010), 25.
11 James Chappel, *Catholic Modern: The Challenge of Totalitarianism and the Remaking of the Church* (Cambridge, MA: Harvard University Press, 2018), 40.
12 Chappel, *Catholic Modern*, 36.
13 Chappel, *Catholic Modern*, 36.
14 David Cayley, *Ivan Illich: In Conversation* (Toronto: Anansi, 1992), 59.
15 Cayley, *Ivan Illich*, 59.

school coursework at the Liceo Scientifico Leonardo da Vinci. At the University of Florence, he studied chemistry under a false name and participated in activities related to the resistance to fascism. Illich said to Cayley in the *In Conversation* interview that he had registered for purely practical reasons: "I got legitimacy by obtaining an ID card, which provided me with a false identity, under the Fascists. It was one little tool which was useful."[16]

In 1944 Illich moved to Rome to continue his studies at the Pontifical Gregorian University, the most prestigious Catholic institution of higher education run by the Jesuits. He was only eighteen when he decided to become a priest. However, it is not clear how he discerned his vocation. There are two general references we know of that are indirect in character but that do not allow a sound inference. One occurred in the interview with Cayley, who prompted Illich by saying: "You said that at twelve you concluded that you would never have children." Illich replied, "I remember it exactly. I walked through the vineyards outside of Vienna. I knew that within days Hitler would be occupying Austria, and I said to myself that, under these circumstances, certain things will happen which will make it impossible for me to give children to these towers down on the island in Dalmatia where my grandfathers and great-grandfathers made children."[17] The second instance we traced is where Todd Hartch mentions a general statement that appears in "The Vanishing Clergyman," included as a chapter in Illich's *Celebration of Awareness*. When discussing renunciation of marriage, Illich refers to the mysterious experience of vocation that we must distinguish from the discursive formulation of reasons to "justify" that decision.[18] The reading of his work leads one to think of a mystical dimension in his way of being. His spirituality was recorded by those who witnessed it in him, and thus there are testimonies of fasts, retreats, austere disciplines, pilgrimages, meditation at a monastery in the Sahara desert during his vacation when he was at the University of Puerto Rico, and his four-month walk from Santiago (Chile) to Caracas (Venezuela) in the winter of 1960–1.[19] It seems that at times he kept some form of moral rigorism that could be related to Jansenism (a sixteenth-century current condemned by the Vatican as heresy, but quite influential). Of relevance

---

16 Cayley, *Ivan Illich*, 81.
17 Cayley, *Ivan Illich*, 76.
18 Ivan Illich, "The Vanishing Clergyman," in *Celebration of Awareness: A Call for Institutional Revolution* (New York: Doubleday, 1971), in particular 75.
19 Francine du Plessix Gray, *Divine Disobedience: Profiles in Catholic Radicalism* (New York: Alfred A. Knopf, 1970), 251.

here is also that after a thirty-day retreat under Jesuit spiritual direction, Illich decided not to become a Jesuit.

Next, as part of our attempt to trace the connections of his formation, the way he dealt with new contexts and ways of seeing the world, and how he negotiated meaning and introduced his ulterior critique of the institutional church and from there moved to a critique of education and the certainties of modernity, we will introduce the complex theological context to which he was exposed during his formation, while he also pursued a degree in history.

The Context: The Magisterium, Emerging Theologies, and Modernity

Illich studied theology at a pontifical university in the 1940s and was ordained as a priest in 1951. He was exposed to an intellectual world in which the repressive policies from the Vatican coexisted with new developments outside the Vatican walls. Indeed, the Vatican's *Magisterium Ecclesiae* (the official teaching of the church) had condemned modernity as heretic in the encyclical *Quanta Cura*, or Condemning Current Errors, of Pius IX (1864) and the appended *Syllabus Errorum*, or The Syllabus of Errors, and in subsequent encyclicals, including *Pascendi Dominici Gregis*, or Feeding the Lord's Flock, by Pius X in 1907.[20] The magisterium kept an anti-modernist position, the intellectual framework of which was known as neo-scholasticism. This lasted until Vatican II. It was an interpretation of Thomism (Thomas Aquinas) mediated by scholastic interpretations of the sixteenth century. It was an Aristotelic theology that defended an objective order of divine events and teachings, and a speculative theology not open to the realities of history.[21] Modernity had created a tension between philosophy and history. Leo XIII's (pope between 1878 and 1903) call for a philosophical foundation for theology

---

20 Pius IX, *Quanta Cura*, Encyclical on Condemning Current Errors (Vatican: The Holy See, 8 December 1864), https://www.papalencyclicals.net/pius09/p9quanta.htm; Pius IX, *Syllabus Errorum*, Encyclical on The Syllabus of Errors (Vatican: The Holy See, 8 December 1864), https://www.papalencyclicals.net/pius09/p9syll.htm; Pius X, *Pascendi Dominici Gregis*, Encyclical on Feeding the Lord's Flock (Vatican: The Holy See, 8 September 1907), http://www.vatican.va/content/pius-x/en/encyclicals/documents/hf_p-x_enc_19070908_pascendi-dominici-gregis.html.

21 Mettepenningen, *Nouvelle théologie*; Michael Attridge, "From Objectivity to Subjectivity: Changes in the 19th and 20th Centuries and Their Impact on Post-Vatican II Theological Education," in *Catholic Education in the Wake of Vatican II*, eds. Rosa Bruno-Jofré and Jon Igelmo Zaldívar (Toronto: University of Toronto Press, 2017).

in order to enter into dialogue with modernity evolved into a "philo-sophical superstructure" that placed modernity as the enemy.[22]

Jürgen Mettepenningen, citing Richard Schaeffler, wrote that "the Church was more interested in modernist deviation from neo-scholastic concepts than modernist ideas as such."[23] In fact, Catholic teachers and professors took from 1910 an anti-modernist oath that practically lasted until the late 1960s. In practice, Catholics took a pragmatic approach to living in a modern world.

The scenario was a bit more complex. Illich did not encounter the so-called modernist crisis of the beginning of the twentieth century, when those theologians who tried to integrate a critical historical method in their theology were persecuted, but he heard the echoes of their analy-sis. He was exposed to the orthodoxy of the magisterium and its anti-modernism, but also to the pluralization of neo-Thomism with its vari-ous tendencies that ran between 1920 and 1950, and of course to *nouvelle théologie*. Illich was influenced by Maritain during his years in Rome in the 1940s and also later in the United States. Maritain used human intu-ition as the key to relativize Thomism and integrated the contemporary culture in his neo-Thomism. He went to Thomas Aquinas and to scho-lastics from the sixteenth and seventeenth centuries – mainly Tomás Caeyatano and Juan de Santo Tomás – and came up with the notion of integral humanism (l'humanisme intégral). The notion, whereby the human person had a natural purpose that would be accomplished through politics and a supernatural purpose to be achieved through religion and ethics, was conveyed in his 1936 book *Integral Humanism*.[24] Thomism served as a foundation for Maritain and was central in Illich's intellectual framework.

Illich put it this way:

> Maritain entered my life quite early and became very important for me while he was ambassador in Rome [1945–8] and had a little seminar there, at the embassy [a time when Maritain had gone through a process of change himself]. He made me go back to another great friend whom I acquired in a way only through him, Aquinas. The Gothic approach, both narrow and precise, and extraordinarily illuminating, which Mari-tain had to the texts of St. Thomas, laid the Thomistic foundations of my entire perceptual mode. I don't know whether, if I submitted myself to the judgement of Thomists, they would accept this, but I experienced

---

22 Mettepenningen, *Nouvelle théologie*, 24.
23 Mettepenningen, *Nouvelle théologie*, 24.
24 Mettepenningen, *Nouvelle théologie*, 25.

Thomism – no, Thomas – as I discovered him through Jacques Maritain, at the architecture which has made me intellectually free to move between Hugh of S. Victor and Kant, between Schutz – or God knows what strange German – and Freud, or, again, into the world of Islam, without getting dispersed.[25]

Maritain, an anti-fascist Catholic, wanted to eliminate anti-Semitism in the church. Maritain, as Chappel wrote, thought the church could come to this on its own by "fully disentangling itself from throne-and-altar fantasies in the name of a more robust, and emancipatory, engagement with the secular world."[26] From the 1920s, there were other neo-Thomist tendencies that went directly to Thomas Aquinas himself and other very early sources: a historical Thomism that returned to Thomas Aquinas as a source of contemporary theology; and a transcendental Thomism stressing continuity with Thomas Aquinas "in the subject's dynamic openness with respect to absolute Being" and in dialogue with modernity.[27] Yet another tendency showed the influence of phenomenology, and some representatives read Thomas Aquinas in light of the phenomenological analysis of consciousness.[28] These developments reached authors who would be protagonists of the *nouvelle théologie*. It was certainly the time from the 1920s onwards of the emergence of phenomenology (Edmund Husserl) and existentialism (Martin Heidegger and Karl Jaspers), whose interpretation of perception and experience of reality influenced Catholic theology and in particular the personalism of Emmanuel Mounier.[29] These tendencies coexisted with neo-scholasticism, the official orthodoxy of the Vatican.

The theological landscape Illich encountered at the time of his formation thus had a diversity of approaches, and anti-modernity took other shapes as well. While medievalists or neo-medievalists had felt in the 1920s that Europe had gone the wrong way with the principles of modernity, others, who were also anti-modernists, thought Catholicism could not be limited to the private sphere, but rather than nostalgic restoration, those theologians wanted to move beyond modernity by "infusing the new spirit of democracy and progress with the ancient ethos of the Church."[30] These theologians, who were neither medievalists

---

25 Cayley, *Ivan Illich*, 150.
26 Chappel, *Catholic Modern*, 152.
27 Mettepenningen, *Nouvelle théologie*, 26.
28 Mettepenningen, *Nouvelle théologie*, 26.
29 Mettepenningen, *Nouvelle théologie*, 27.
30 Chappel, *Catholic Modern*, 43.

nor modernists, were described as ultramodern.[31] One of the major representatives was Waldemar Gurian (1902–54), professor of political science at University of Notre Dame in Indiana. Together, Gurian and Maritain were the major representatives of a change in the interpretation of Catholicism and its place in modern society, particularly in the 1930s.[32] Maritain attacked "political theology" – the notion of an integralist society in which the line between church and state fades away.[33] This interpretation would be a third way alternative to the materialism of individualist liberalism and totalitarian communism. The critique of the state form that survived in the 1930s vanished in the 1940s; both civil society Catholics and corporatist Catholics, in spite of their differences, developed forms of personalism and anti-totalitarianism.[34] In the 1940s, Christian democracy would be an expression of the third way, mentioned above. Both Gurian and Maritain would become Cold War warriors.

Illich was also exposed to the development of the movement known as *nouvelle théologie*, although, as we will see, he did not define himself as such in 1950, during the confrontation of *nouvelle théologie* theologians with the Vatican. The starting point of this challenging theological approach is placed in the article written by Dominican Yves Congar entitled "Déficit de la théologie."[35] This current, embedded in the French-speaking parts of Europe, was a precursor of Vatican II. The theologians involved in this movement brought history to theology, were critical of neo-scholasticism as a straitjacket not open to history or to reality, and questioned its speculative theology. The *nouvelle théologie* connected in its various phases with the historical reality of faith and daily life, and favoured a positive theology grounded on induction rather than deduction.[36] Illich was in touch with many of these theologians,

---

31 Chappel, *Catholic Modern*, 43.
32 See Waldemar Gurian Letters received from Jacques Maritain (ZAN), University of Notre Dame Archives (UNDA), Notre Dame, IN 46556. There are twenty-nine letters. The University of Notre Dame Archives are available at http://archives .nd.edu/. See also James Chappel, "Slaying the Leviathan: Catholicism and the Rebirth of European Conservatism, 1920–1950" (PhD diss., Columbia University, 2012).
33 Samuel Moyn, "Jacques Maritain, Christian New Order, and the Origins of Human Rights," in *Intercultural Dialogue and Human Rights*, eds. Luigi Bonanante, Roberto Papini, and William Sweet (Washington, DC: Council for Research in Values and Philosophy, 2011), 4.
34 Moyn, "Jacques Maritain," 4.
35 Yves Congar, "Déficit de la théologie," *Sept*, 18 January 1935.
36 Mettepenningen, *Nouvelle théologie*, 10.

and he mentioned some of them in his writings, as was the case with Edward Schillebeeckx, a promoter of the "theology of reality."[37] Schillebeeckx expounded a theology oriented towards the sources of faith and characterized by historical-critical exegesis and an understanding of spiritual tradition.

After the war, Illich enrolled at the University of Salzburg to obtain legal residency status in Austria. He attended classes at the Philosophischen Institut der Theologischen Fakultät with historian Albert Auer on medieval theologies and suffering, and also with Michel Muechlin. Auer, an old Benedictine monk, would direct Illich's thesis on the philosophical foundations of the historiography of Arnold Joseph Toynbee.[38] Illich remembered his three-hour walks with him along the Salzach, after which they would go for a beer and dry bread.[39] The thesis was later critiqued for not dealing in a satisfactory manner with the relationship of science and religion, for not engaging in a criticism of religion nor the notion of civilization, and for including "some superficialities and contradictions."[40] However, Illich does critically explore in the thesis Toynbee's understanding of how the personality influences society, and he moves the argument to a relationship between the field of influence and a novel model that shapes relations that make up an institution.[41] He seemed inclined to explore the relationship between individuals and institutions.

Meanwhile, he had continued at the Pontifical Gregorian University where he completed a master's degree in philosophy and theology – a theology, in his words, "of the most traditional and, if you want, somewhat obscurantist type," but one that demanded a foundation in the Fathers of the church, the Scholastics, and the spiritual masters.[42] He also studied informally with Maritain, as mentioned before, and prepared himself to be ordained. The ordination took place in 1951, at which time he had finished his doctoral degree at Salzburg as well. While at the Pontifical Gregorian University he wrote about Romano Guardini,

---

37 Edward Schillebeeckx, *De sacramentele heilseconomie* (Antwerp: 't Groeit, 1951); Edward Schillebeeckx, *Jesus, An Experimental Christology* (London: Collins, 1979).

38 Ivan Illich, "Die philosophischen Grundlagen der Geschichtsschreibung bei Arnold Joseph Toynbee [The Philosophical Foundations of History Writing According to Arnold Joseph Toynbee]" (PhD diss., University of Salzburg, 1951).

39 Cayley, *Ivan Illich*, 82.

40 Helmut Woll, "Anmerkungen zur dissertation von Ivan Illich über Arnold Joseph Toynbee," *The International Journal of Illich Studies* 5, no. 1 (2016): 44–56.

41 Woll, "Anmerkungen zur dissertation," 52–3.

42 David Cayley, *The Rivers North of the Future: The Testament of Ivan Illich as Told to David Cayley*, foreword by Charles Taylor (Toronto: Anansi, 2005), 142.

and this is telling because this theologian understood the church as a community of believers, as "the people of God on its way." This understanding is particularly evident in Guardini's book *Vom sinn der kirche* (Of the Meaning of the Church).[43] The supernatural character of the church gained relevance with the notion of the church as the mystical body of Christ being advanced by Belgian Jesuit Émile Mersch.[44] It is interesting that when talking of ecclesiology, Illich said: "One can look at the Church as a mystery of faith, and ecclesiology as the task of studying the object of faith which calls itself Church and considers itself to be the mystical body of Christ, with 'mystical' meaning communal."[45]

Illich developed an eclectic vision of the church and a consistent critique of modernity and the role of the state that we can connect like complex threads in a piece of knitting to various conceptions with which he was in touch from an early age. He produced an Illichean critique that was tainted by his own living experience and the interaction of his intellectual tools and the way he chose to interpret his world. There was, however, an axial line guiding his interpretation.

A central question guiding this narrative is, what were the lines of thought in the pragmatic approach leading his intuitions that led to Illich's critique of the structures and pillars sustaining the beliefs of modern societies? We have in mind here the multidimensional readings we can undertake of the apophatic *Deschooling Society*.

From Rome to the United States: 1951

In 1951, the year Illich became ordained and finished his doctoral degree, he met Cardinal Francis Spellman, archbishop of New York, in Rome, and decided to leave Rome and go to the United States. Cardinal Giovanni Montini (later Pope Paul VI) had wished for him to enter the Accademia dei Nobili Ecclesiastici and be trained for a career as a church diplomat.[46] Instead, Illich decided to leave Rome because, he stated, he did not want to be part of the papal bureaucracy. Another reason he gave was that the magisterium's theological positioning was separated from world issues. In fact, in 1950, Pope Pius XII had promulgated the encyclical *Humani Generis*, or Of the

---

43 Romano Guardini, *Vom Sinn der Kirche* [Of the Meaning of the Church] (Mainz: Matthias Grünewald, 1922).
44 Mettepenningen, *Nouvelle théologie*, 27.
45 Cayley, *Rivers North of the Future*, 142.
46 Hartch, *The Prophet of Cuernavaca*, 6.

Human Race, "concerning some false opinions threatening to undermine the foundations of Catholic doctrine."[47] The Cold War was on.

On this point, later, when discussing with Cayley the reason why he abandoned the Vatican II Council (1962–5) and his work with Belgium Cardinal Suenens, Illich recalled: "I said to him, 'I am leaving now. Yesterday you proved to me that this Council is incapable of facing the issues which count, while trying hard to remain traditional.'"[48] He was referring to the failure of the council to condemn governments for keeping atomic bombs.[49] A historical reading of the context in which Illich acted makes things a bit more complicated than his self-portraying explanation.

We have traced Illich's own positioning on the theological debate when he was at the Vatican. At the time, the theologians of the *nouvelle théologie*, among them Henri de Lubac, Jean Daniélou, and the Fourvière Jesuits, were engaged in a fierce struggle with neo-scholastics and the Vatican. They were critical of neo-scholasticism. *Nouvelle théologie* was a powerful movement that would reach a high point of influence at the Vatican II Council. Meanwhile, *Humani Generis*, mentioned above, ran parallel with *Pascendi Dominici Gregis* (1907) in its orthodox positioning and its anti-modernity, and although it does not mention the *nouvelle théologie*, it condemns thirteen matters referred to as "new." As Mettepenningen wrote, *Humani Generis* clearly rejected the *nouvelle théologie*, and the pope attacked historicism for placing too much emphasis on particular facts.[50] The pope opposed consideration of a living tradition as a component of theology, while *nouvelle* theologians wanted to cross boundaries and move towards a historically oriented Thomism; later, they moved beyond that. Illich did not refer to this dimension of the encyclical and avoided participation in the debate. Instead, he separated himself from the confrontation and from the Vatican, left aside the idea of becoming a bureaucrat in the Vatican, and moved to the United States to do a postdoctoral thesis on alchemy in the work of Albert the Great at Princeton, where there were good library sources and where Maritain was teaching.[51] He had a few

---

47 Pius XII, *Humani Generis* [Of the Human Race], Encyclical (Vatican: The Holy See, 12 August 1950), http://www.vatican.va/content/pius-xii/en/encyclicals /documents/hf_p-xii_enc_12081950_humani-generis.html.

48 Cayley, *Rivers North of the Future*, 7.

49 David Cayley, *Ivan Illich in Conversation* (Toronto: Anansi, 1992), 100–1.

50 Mettepenningen, *Nouvelle théologie*, 35.

51 David Cayley, "Part Moon, Part Travelling Salesman; Conversations with Ivan Illich," *Ideas*, 21 and 28 November 1989, 5, 12, and 19 December 1989, *The Canadian Broadcasting Corporation*, transcripts, 1.

contacts in the United States. On one hand, there were his family contacts related to his late well-connected grandfather, Regenstreif, in New York, and on the other, the archbishop of New York, Cardinal Francis Spellman, whom he had met in Rome not long before. Spellman took Illich to his archdiocese in New York in 1951, when Illich was twenty-five years old, and placed him in Washington Heights, New York, a conservative Irish parish.

Illich's stay in New York defined his future work. He recounted to David Cayley that on the first evening in New York, he heard about the Puerto Rican community through friends of his grandfather, who told him that they had to move out of the neighbourhood because all "those people" were moving there. And the Black cook then said that her family, old Southern Blacks, had to move from Harlem because Puerto Ricans were coming in.[52] Illich said, "So I spent the next two days up in the barrio beneath the tracks of New York Central, where they had their market, and afterwards went to Cardinal Spellman's office and asked for an assignment to a Puerto Rican parish. And that's how I got stuck in New York."[53] He went as an assistant priest to the Incarnation Church parish, located on St. Nicholas Ave., at 175th Street, close to the George Washington Bridge.

We are not trying to provide a biography. Our purpose is to simply point out the experiences in Illich's life and the choices he made that would set the experiential context for his critique of the church as institution, and from there for his shift to schooling at the end of the 1960s – in particular, on the monopolization of education by the state and a critique of schooling within the framework of modernity. We will explore how this critique was in great measure grounded in his intellectual background and his medievalist ethos, even as we agree with Cayley, who wrote that "Illich's sudden fascination with the Puerto Ricans was to shape the whole subsequent direction of his life," a life that was also marked by high-level contacts.[54] Illich used his privileged social background to cultivate important social and political relations in New York within the church and beyond. The relationship with Cardinal Spellman would define his positioning in the church and give him connections, and it would have a place in the discussion of the apophatic *Deschooling Society* that came after Spellman's death.

---

52 Cayley, "Part Moon," 1.
53 Cayley, "Part Moon," 1.
54 Cayley, "Part Moon," 3.

Sojourn in New York and the Move to Puerto Rico: The Early Relationship with Francis Cardinal Spellman and Implications for Illich's Future Work

Cardinal Spellman responded immediately to Illich's request and moved him from Washington Heights to the Incarnation parish. There, the older immigrants of Jewish, Italian, and Irish origin were reacting to the Puerto Ricans. Illich joined other young priests, including Joseph Fitzpatrick, not surprisingly a Jesuit, to make the local church and institutions culturally sensitive to the needs of the new immigrants, who incidentally were US citizens.[55] Illich, a polyglot who grew up at the intersection of various European cultures, was sensitive to cultural matters. He went to the local library and worked together with them to build a library in Spanish for the Puerto Rican children. Illich became involved in the life of the community, which very few priests did at the time, and people perceived his devotion when he said Mass.[56] Illich, who had learned Spanish, as Joseph Fitzpatrick said, was revered.[57] He wanted to minister in a spiritual and religious style that would make sense to the community. In this he was not far from theological developments taking place outside the Vatican. The experience at the Incarnation parish and his concern with cultural sensitivity made up the first link in his journey that would take him to the experience in Cuernavaca. Spellman himself worked hard to integrate Puerto Ricans into the US Catholic Church and urged the celebration of their national festival, the Fiesta of San Juan, with Masses in the cathedral as well as outdoor celebrations. It was also a political issue. Illich visited prestigious Catholic colleges, such as the College of New Rochelle, located in New Rochelle, New York, to get support. This is where he met a young woman who would later become Mother David Serna (Anne) OSB, who recalled the famous "cuartito" they rented: "Illich wanted Puerto Rican immigrants to have a place to gather, [so] we chipped in and rented a one bedroom apartment [and] we invited people and the kids, families, [and it was a] small outreach."[58] She graduated in 1956 and went to Puerto Rico to teach for a year, where she met Illich again.

---

55 Cayley, "Part Moon," 3.

56 Cayley, "Part Moon," 3.

57 Cayley, "Part Moon," 3.

58 R.M. David Serna, Abbess Emerita, OSB, Abbey of Regina Laudis, 273 Flanders Road, Bethlehem, CT. Her father was Peruvian and her mother English. She participated in the activities of the parish between 1952 and 1956. She had met Illich

Illich recalled that while in New York, he experienced, "one of the greatest moments of my life, a moment when I was both proud of myself and humbled as never before or afterwards came when Jacques Maritain had a heart attack while teaching at Princeton. I was then a twenty-six-year-old guy working as a parish priest among Puerto Ricans in New York, and I got a call from the Institute for Advanced Studies asking me to take over the seminar Maritain had been conducting on Thomas's *De Esse et Essentia.*"[59]

Illich was overwhelmed with the offer because Maritain had introduced him to Thomas Aquinas, an author who remained important to Illich, as he saw him, in retrospect, "both as a counterweight to the Franciscan tradition, and in a biographical sense."[60]

The relationship with Spellman is as fundamental as it is unexplainable in Illich's trajectory. After the Second World War, Spellman was one of the most important figures representing and promoting conservative positions of the Catholic Church in the United States. William V. Shannon wrote, "Spellman was deeply reactionary in his theology and secular politics. He was, for example, hostile to ecumenism, liturgical reform (including saying the mass in English) and all intellectual attempts to take account of the truth that the church actually thrives in America's pluralistic and officially secular society."[61] Spellman was known, beyond his public conservative positions already mentioned, for his relationship with the CIA, his predatory sexual behaviour with young men, as well as his strong stances on morality and his critique of homosexuality. His relationship with Spellman is an important point of reference to explain Illich's movement away from the critique of the church as institution to the apophatic critique of schooling and other modern institutions.

Spellman provided unfaltering support to Illich until days before his death in 1967, even when Illich was involved in a strong conflict with the Vatican, specifically with the Sacred Congregation for the Doctrine of the Faith. We begin here with providing some initial landmarks in Illich's relationship with Spellman and its benefits for Illich until the

---

when he gave a talk to the students at College of New Rochelle, a private Catholic college, where she had been introduced by one of her high school teachers given her poor background. Rosa Bruno-Jofré interviewed her in August 2017 in the monastery.

59 Cayley, *Rivers North of the Future*, 67.
60 Cayley, *Rivers North of the Future*, 67.
61 William V. Shannon, "Guileless and Machiavellian," *The New York Times*, 2 October 1984, https://www.nytimes.com/1984/10/28/books/guileless-and-machiavellian .html.

cardinal's death in 1967. In 1952 Spellman recommended Illich as an instructor in the Faculty of Political Science at Fordham University.[62] That same year, Spellman appointed Illich as coordinator of the Hispano American Office of the Archdioceses of New York. In 1956 Spellman recommended that the thirty-year-old Illich be appointed vicerector of the University of Puerto Rico, and he also made him director of the Instituto de Comunicación Intercultural, also in Puerto Rico. In August 1957 John XXIII, following a recommendation from Spellman, named Illich Chaplain of His Holiness, a title that made him a monsignor as well, at thirty-one years of age. This meteoric career was explained by Illich's intellectual talent. However, testimonies from priests contemporary to Illich, who also worked with Spellman, can move us in a more complex analytical direction. A paragraph from *The Stranger is Our Own* by Jesuit Joseph Fitzpatrick provides a foundation to broaden the interpretation. Fitzpatrick wrote:

> There is no doubt that Illich had extraordinary influence with the Cardinal. When Illich came to New York, he came with glowing credentials from people in Rome. Cardinal Spellman immediately sensed the importance of this. But beyond this, on two occasions, the details of which I never knew, Illich intervened to save the Cardinal's embarrassment by events that had happened in the archdioceses. Illich, with his consummate diplomacy, straightened things out before the Cardinal would have become involved. Thus, from the very beginning, the Cardinal knew that Illich had extraordinary gifts which could be helpful to him. At the same time, Illich knew that Spellman's involvement in the Hispanic apostolate was critical. Spellman's confidence in him enabled Illich to bring ideas and suggestions to him and to get support for his proposal for the Hispanic apostolate. What became clear later on was that Spellman became Illich's great protector.[63]

We know now that the cardinal was involved in many improper and unwanted situations with young men. The critical review of John Cooney's *The American Pope: The Life and Times of Francis Cardinal Spellman* by William Shannon, for the *New York Times Book Review*,[64] generated

---

62 Matthew J. O'Meagher, "Catholicism, Reform, and Development in Latin America, 1959–67" (PhD diss., partial fulfilment, Duke University, 1994), 371.

63 Joseph P. Fitzpatrick, *The Stranger Is Our Own: Reflections on the Journey of Puerto Rican Migrants* (Kansas City: Sheed & Ward, 1996), 28.

64 John Cooney, *The American Pope: The Life and Times of Francis Cardinal Spellman* (New York: Times Books, 1984); William V. Shannon, "Guileless and Machiavellian,"

a strong reaction from William Hart McNichols, S.J., who wrote in a letter to the *New York Times*:

> William V. Shannon states, "prurient interest in the sex lives of public figures serves no useful purpose. What matters about them is what they did in the public sphere." In the light of the present climate of discrimination and fear created in the Roman Catholic Church for homosexuals and lesbians, this statement is ironic and terribly naïve. If a homosexual man was considered (and could be considered) worthy to shepherd the Archdiocese of New York City, then other homosexuals and lesbians should be considered worthy to work in such places as day care centers, etc. Cardinal Spellman's sex life does not matter, but [his] homosexuality does indeed matter. It matters to thousands of people whose jobs, relationships and whose very lives are threatened because of their sexuality, all the while being forced to view and eat the hypocrisy of their church. And it enrages people that church men and women can retain their jobs, hiding behind their clerical and religious status while their own people suffer persecution, disease and discrimination.[65]

Incidentally, the publisher of Cooney's book edited the book, and Spellman's homosexuality and his behaviour were reduced from a few pages to a paragraph. It reads: "For years rumors abounded about Cardinal Spellman being a homosexual. As a result, many felt – and continue to feel – that Spellman the public moralist may well have been a contradiction of the man of the flesh."[66] Journalist Michelangelo Signorele described Spellman as "one of the most notorious, powerful and sexually voracious homosexuals in the American Catholic Church's history."[67]

We are not able to fully explain the reasons for Spellman's protection beyond the inferences of Illich having a hand in solving the cardinal's personal problems. However, this protection helps to explain Illich's

---

The New York Times, 28 October 1984, https://www.nytimes.com/1984/10/28/books/guileless-and-machiavellian.html. A version of this review appeared in print on 28 October 1984, in section 7, p. 11 of the national edition with the headline: GUILELESS AND MACHIAVELLIAN.

65 William Hart McNichols, S.J., "Letter to the Editor of the New York Times," 25 November 1984, section 7, 30, https://www.nytimes.com/1984/11/25/books/l-cardinal-spellman-and-the-public-106570.html. See Michelangelo Signorile, *Queer in America: Sex, the Media, and the Closets of Power* (Madison: University of Wisconsin Press, 2003, extended edition), 434.

66 Cooney, *The American Pope*, 109.

67 Michelangelo Signorile, "Cardinal Spellman's Dark Legacy," *New York Press*, 23 April 2002, http://www.msignorile.com/articles_spellman.htm.

appointments as well as simply confusing or unclear situations, such as the freedom and financial support he enjoyed in Cuernavaca – in spite of his radical views and his change of direction in his critical writing, in which he moved away from his acidic critique of the church as institution after losing Spellman's protection. We will come back to this point.

While in New York, Illich built a relationship with Dorothy Dohen, editor of *Integrity*, a popular monthly magazine founded in 1946 by lay Catholics. It aimed at reorienting people's lives towards Christ. The magazine is described as a medium for having a way to critique the official church by taking its teaching more seriously and more literally while trying to avoid becoming a middle-class magazine.[68] By the mid-1950s, Dohen had given the publication a new editorial direction, and under the influence of Illich, the magazine brought the issue of immigration to a wider audience in a special issue of *Integrity* that focused on Puerto Ricans and the church in July 1955.[69] Illich published articles in this magazine that had a rather conservative theological tone, such as "Sacred Virginity" and, to an extent, "Rehearsal for Death," as well as a mystical component.[70] He argued in a June 1955 article, "The American Parish," that the parishioners did not find in parishes what they sought, writing that "Criticism of the parish will thus become an examination of conscience for everybody who engages in it: layman, priest, and outsider alike. And if it is not criticism of the clergy or the laity, but of the institution itself, it will mostly revolve around the idea that the protective parish is a thing of the past almost everywhere in this country."[71] He was thinking of the protective parish as the centre of the community as in medieval times; his language here was also inspired by Belgium Jesuit Émile Mersch's vision that the life Jesus lived in Judea and the life Jesus now prolongs in the church are not separate lives. Mersch wrote: "The historical Christ is the same as the mystical Christ; his historical

---

68 Patrick Allitt, *Catholic Converts: British and American Intellectuals Turn to Rome* (Ithaca, NY: Cornell University Press, 1997), 318. The editor of *Integrity* was Carol Robinson. In 1952 Dorothy Dohen became the editor; she was a friend of Illich. The magazine at one point had 15,000 subscribers.

69 James Terence Fisher, *The Catholic Counterculture 1933–1962* (Chapel Hill: University of North Carolina Press, 1989).

70 Ivan Illich, "Sacred Virginity," *Integrity*, October 1955, in Ivan Illich, *The Powerless Church and Other Selected Writings, 1955–1985* (University Park: Pennsylvania State University Press, 2018), 32–5; Ivan Illich, "Rehearsal for Death," *Integrity*, March 1956, in Illich, *The Powerless Church*, 4–10.

71 Ivan Illich, "The American Parish," *Integrity*, June 1955, in Illich, *The Powerless Church*, 5–16.

life was already his mystical life."[72] This ecclesiology was adopted by the Vatican, and in 1943, Pope Pius XII promulgated the encyclical *Mystici Corporis Christi*, or The Mystical Body of Christ, emphasizing the invisible nature of the church, although the encyclical kept the authority of the magisterium.[73] The point here is that Illich's critique of the church's inability to adapt culturally to the Puerto Rican community is related in the June article to the notion of the church as the mystical body of Christ, language Illich used. It is not a critique of the church as an institution at large at this point, but of the institution that had lost its protective character as it was in medieval times. An interesting phrase leads us to a theme he would develop later in relation to the parable of the Good Samaritan: "The parish must become and is becoming in the consciousness of the Catholic the spiritual home of all those who live within its boundaries – even if many do not know where their home is. This is happening all over. The Legion of Mary is growing, these are laymen who consecrate two evenings a week to the conversion of their neighbor."[74] It was a way to infuse the culture with Catholic values. Here we find some seeds that would lead to Illich's critique of the institutional church and eventually other forms of institutionalization, such as schooling.

Illich was part of the circle of *The Commonweal Magazine*, a progressive journal critical of orthodox positions, where Jacques Maritain, Dorothy Day, Thomas Merton, and Hannah Arendt published articles. Illich was also familiar with currents that questioned US imperialism and the position of the US church in relation to Latin America. The magazine represented a personalist tendency with an emphasis on the subjectivity of the person and the notion of Christians being in communion with others. This Catholicism of engagement embodied an indignation over US materialism and individualism. The thinking of Emmanuel Mounier (1905–50), author of *Révolution personnaliste et communautaire*,[75] and the notion that Catholic principles could be infused in the culture were present. These ideas move the authors back

---

72 Émile Mersch, S.J., "La vie historique de Jesus et sa vie mystique," *Nouvelle Revue Théologique* 60, no. 1 (January 1933): 5–20.

73 Mettepenningen, *Nouvelle théologie*, 27; see also Pius XII, *Mystici Corporis Christi*, Encyclical on the Mystical Body of Christ (Vatican: The Holy See, 29 June 1943), http://www.vatican.va/content/pius-xii/en/encyclicals/documents/hf_p-xii _enc_29061943_mystici-corporis-christi.html.

74 Illich, "The American Parish," 12.

75 Emmanuel Mounier, *Révolution personnaliste et communinautaire* (Paris: Fernand Aubier, Editions Montaigne, 1934).

to ways Illich dealt with modernity while questioning it, by keeping an anti-modernist approach.

As we mentioned before, in 1956 Spellman recommended that the thirty-year-old Illich be appointed vice-rector of the University of Puerto Rico and also director of the Instituto de Comunicación Intercultural. We don't have elements to explain the decision or the good relationship Illich had with Spellman, whose ultra-conservative positions and predatory behaviour, discussed before, were well known, but Illich's stay in Puerto Rico provides clues about his evolving notion of the missionary, his future work in Cuernavaca, and his immersion into schooling. As cases in point, his relationship with Leopold Kohr, the Austrian political scientist who asked Illich to challenge the very concept of development, and Everett Reimer, a critic of schooling, would lead to transformational changes in Illich's thinking and action.

The Experience in Puerto Rico: Defining Illich's Thinking and Praxis on Education and Schooling

Young Illich went to Puerto Rico in November 1956 as vice-rector of the Pontificia Universidad Católica de Puerto Rico in Ponce. He was in that position until 1960. Following Joseph Fitzpatrick, S.J., who worked with Illich, the team working with the Puerto Ricans saw the need to create some kind of bridge between the Latin world and the United States; Puerto Rico was the natural place to begin, and Illich was the right person. Illich then told Spellman that he was willing to go to Puerto Rico and that he would start the Institute of Intercultural Communication.[76]

The Institute – a summer institute – aimed at training priests and religious to work in an intercultural environment, particularly in the Spanish ghettos and with Puerto Ricans in New York, and at teaching them Spanish. As Fitzpatrick wrote, "the training at the Institute was designed to help the mainland clergy and religious – most of them from middle-class Irish, German or Italian backgrounds – to appreciate the Puerto Ricans for what they are, to form them spiritually and religiously in accordance with their own deep religious values and sentiments, rather than remake them on the American religious pattern."[77]

The workshops at the Institute combined intensive study of spoken Spanish with field experience and the study of Puerto Rican cultural expressions and history. The participants had decided to spend their

---

76 Cayley, "Part Moon," 4.
77 J.P. Fitzpatrick, "What is He Getting At?" *America* (25 March 1967), 444.

lives with the city's poor.[78] Illich believed that in the process of learning a new language, the adult can go through a deep experience of poverty, weakness, and dependence on the good will of another. It is interesting that silence in the form of meditation, a silent prayer, was practised every evening. In "The Eloquence of Silence," he classified the types of silence, often displaying a misogynist tone, not surprising in the Catholic context of the time and in the context of Illich's Thomism:

> the silence of the pure listener, of womanly passivity; the silence through which the message of the other becomes "he in us", the silence of deep interest. It is threatened by another silence: the silence of indifference, the silence of disinterest which assumes that there is nothing I want or can receive through the communication to the other. This this is the ominous silence of the wife who woodenly listens to her husband relating the little things he so earnestly wants to tell her. It is the silence of the Christian who reads the gospel with the attitude that he knows it backward and forward. It is the silence of the stone – dead because it is unrelated to life. It is the silence of the missioner who never understood the miracle of a foreigner whose listening is a greater testimony of love than that of another who speaks. The man who shows us that he knows the rhythm of our silence is much closer to us than one who thinks that he knows how to speak.[79]

At this time, he also wrote for the workshops "Spiritual Poverty and the Missionary Character," a rich spiritual piece. Illich wrote: "The acquiescence to foreign cultural norms of behavior and taboos, besides being a necessary utilitarian accommodation and a mark of delicacy and charitable toleration, can become an imitation of the Incarnation in a unique form of contemplation: to be like the Lord in His poverty and to be so for no further reason but love."[80]

What is missionary poverty? In Illich's words, "The missioner must go even further into an area of detachment from himself [sic] which suggests calling 'missionary poverty', an intimate mystical imitation

---

78 Ivan Illich, "The Eloquence of Silence," in *Celebration of Awareness: A Call for Institutional Reform* (Garden City, NY: Double Day Anchor Book, 1971). Also published as "Missionary Silence," typescript, 1960, published in *The Church, Change, and Development*, ed. Fred Eychaner (Chicago: Urban Training Center Press, 1970), 120–5.

79 Ivan Illich, "The Eloquence of Silence," in Ivan Illich, *Celebration of Awareness* (New York: Anchor Books, Doubleday, 1971), 32–3.

80 Ivan Illich, "Spiritual Poverty and the Missionary Character," in Illich, *The Powerless Church*, 55. Originally published with the title "Missionary Poverty," in *The Catholic Messenger*, 19 October 1961, 5–6.

of Christ in His Incarnation. From its organization around the acquisi-
tion of this special aspect of the beatitude of poverty corresponding to
the task of the missioner every attempt at missionary formation will
receive unity and deep meaning."[81] Here Illich advanced the notion of
the missionary that he fully developed in the centres in Cuernavaca,
Mexico.

Illich's experience in Puerto Rico represented a turning point in his
personal and intellectual life. He became involved with the first "great
secular bureaucracy," not only as vice-rector of the university but as a
member of the board that governed Puerto Rico's education system.
He was compelled to think of compulsory schooling in Puerto Rico,
and it did not take long for him to see that it constituted "structured
injustice." It was here that he was exposed to new conceptual tools and
that he started to question "development," "human resources," and
"manpower planning." Illich was also involved in the newly established manpower qualifications planning board of the government. He
later wrote:

> I was deeply upset by the philosophical ambiguities into which planning,
> not of the Church, but of something called qualified manpower was lea-
> ding me ... So on my next visit to the mainland I went to see Professor
> Maritain, who had earlier guided my studies on the history of the practice
> and theory of virtue in the Christian West. How could I fit "planning" into
> the traditional system of responsible habits within which I had learned to
> think? I had great difficulty in explaining to the old man the meaning of the
> term that I was using: planning was not accounting, nor was it legislation,
> nor a kind of scheduling of trains. We took a tea on his veranda. It was to
> be my last visit with him. I was delighted to look at his beautiful face, close
> to death, transparent, like one of the patriarchs in a Gothic stained glass
> window. The cup in his hand was shaking. Then, finally, he put it down,
> looking disturbed, and said: "Is not planning, which you talk about, a sin,
> a new species within the vices which grow out of presumption?" He made
> me understand that in thinking about humans as resources that can be
> managed, a new certitude about human nature would be brought into
> existence surreptitiously.[82]

These thoughts had relevance within the context of the time, giving meaning to the concepts under examination, as we will explain.

---

81 Illich, "Spiritual Poverty," 57.
82 Illich, *In the Mirror of the Past*, 221–2.

However, as a reader, one cannot leave aside the way the church man-
aged people and their subjectivities for centuries with the presumption
of truth; the Middle Ages, so much admired by Illich, provides prime
examples.

Nonetheless, we can find here in this paragraph grounding for the critique of the church as one of the corrupting institutions, and of its relations with US programs with Latin America, including the Alliance for
Progress, and of overall interventionism in the name of anti-communism.
The church was loosening its spiritual role. Illich questioned the power
of management to name norms of health, education, and medicine and
to create social contexts in which the "values" (in reference to norms)
are experienced as a need and in turn are translated as an entitlement.[83]

While in Puerto Rico, Illich surrounded himself with people whose
direct experiences and critical thinking of matters of development and
education would help him develop understandings of new issues, such
as development and the role of education. At the core was the issue of
institutionalization.

> After just one year as vice-chancellor of a university in Puerto Rico, in 1957
> I and a few others wanted to question the development ideology to which
> Kennedy no less than Castro subscribed. I put all the money I had – today
> the equivalent of the prize you just gave me – into the purchase of a one
> room wooden shack in the mountains that overlook the Caribbean. With
> three friends I wanted a place of study in which every use of the pronoun
> "nos-otros" would truthfully refer back to the four of "us", and be acces-
> sible to our guests as well; I wanted to practice the rigor that would keep
> us far from the "we" that invokes the security found in the shadow of an
> academic discipline: we as "sociologists", "economists" and so forth. As
> one of us, Charlie Rosario, put it: "All departments smell – of disinfec-
> tants, at their best; and poisoned sterilized aura." "La casita" on the route
> to Adjuntas soon became so obnoxious that I had to leave the Island.[84]

One of those friends was, as mentioned before, Leopold Kohr, whose
thinking can be traced in Illich's positioning vis-à-vis the US presence
in Latin America, the church, and education, among other issues. As
Illich wrote, Kohr had a vision of a "decent common life predicated

---

83   Illich, *In the Mirror of the Past*, 222.
84   Ivan Illich, "The Cultivation of Conspiracy," in *The Challenges of Ivan Illich*, ed. Lee
     Hoinacki and Carl Mitcham (New York: State University of New York Press, 2002),
     237. http://www.davidtinapple.com/illich/1998_Illich-Conspiracy.PDF.

in modesty, not plenty."[85] Kohr, who inspired his student E.F. Schumacher's famous phrase "small is beautiful," thought that "the truth of beauty and goodness is not a matter of size, nor even of dimensions of intensity, but of proportion."[86] Kohr was a professor of political science at the University of Puerto Rico between 1955 and 1973, a time when "Operation Bootstrap," an economic development scheme in social engineering, was in effect. He questioned not only the policies but the concept of development itself. As Illich wrote, "he identified conditions under which the Good became mired down in things that are scarce. Therefore he worked to subvert conventional economic wisdom, no matter how advanced."[87]

Two words in Illich's view reveal Kohr's thought: *verhältnismäßigkeit*, which means proportionality, or, more precisely, the appropriateness of a relationship, and *gewiss*, translated as "certain," as when one says, "in a certain way."[88] Illich wrote, "To consider what is appropriate or fitting in a certain place leads one directly into reflection on beauty and goodness. The truth of one's resulting judgement will be primarily moral, not economic."[89] Kohr rejected the idea of progress that was linked to the idea of consumption and the exploitation of nature and questioned the very concept of development and economic planning. For Kohr, truth of beauty and goodness was not a matter of size but of proportion.[90] These are ideas that Illich would develop on his own journey.

One of the other three friends was Everett Reimer, a US civil servant working for governor Luis Muñoz Marín as a consultant to the Secretariat of Education on the Committee on Human Resources of the Commonwealth of Puerto Rico.[91] Reimer's work was to evaluate the expansion of schooling and its implications, including the impact on

---

85 Ivan Illich, "The Wisdom of Leopold Kohr," *Bulletin of Science, Technology & Society* 17, no. 4 (1997): 157–65, quotation on 157.
86 Illich, "The Wisdom of Leopold Kohr," 157.
87 Illich, "The Wisdom of Leopold Kohr," 157.
88 Illich, "The Wisdom of Leopold Kohr," 158.
89 Illich, "The Wisdom of Leopold Kohr," 158.
90 Illich, "The Wisdom of Leopold Kohr," 157.
91 Reimer had been an advisor to state and federal agencies and had worked for the Atomic Energy Commission. He had done some work with universities, including the Survey Research Center at the University of Michigan, the Washington Research Center of the Maxwell School, and the University of Syracuse. In 1962, he left Puerto Rico and moved to Washington, DC, to work in the office coordinating the Alliance for Progress. In 1964 Reimer went back to Puerto Rico as advisor to the Secretary of Education, Ángel Quintero.

the creation of skilled labour, the social problems emerging, as well as benefits and opportunities.[92] Reimer developed a critical view of the social functionality of schooling and realized the dysfunctionality of schooling for individual development – issues he would further develop in *School Is Dead*. In his thinking, "education, in its more important aspects, occurs to and within the individual in many still rather mysterious ways."[93] He found empirical evidence in Puerto Rico that "children whose home had given them an educational advantage, stay longer in school, while the poor children tend to drop earlier."[94] This was an issue under discussion in the early 1960s that would become central during President Johnson's war on poverty and that was in the foundations of the Head Start programs.

Illich wrote in the Introduction to *Deschooling Society*: "I owe my interest in public education to Everett Reimer. Until we first met in Puerto Rico in 1958, I had never questioned the value of extending obligatory schooling to all people."[95] Illich recalled early in the 2000s that in a conversation with Reimer the question "what is schooling?" came up; they both looked at the institution in formal terms, leaving out people's intentions with regard to education. They concluded that the school was an agency that gathered people for cycles, each one designed to eliminate more and more people in the process of gaining social privilege.[96] An interesting point here is that, as per Illich's recollection, he and Reimer soon found common interests and many parallels in the problems of the church and school. After the conflict with the Vatican and the death of his protector, Illich would turn from a critique of the church to a critique of schooling as an apophatic exercise.

Inspired by the conversations with Reimer, Illich asked for data to figure out what schools were doing in Puerto Rico. After ten years of school development in Puerto Rico, half of the students who came from the poorer families had a one-in-three chance of finishing five years of elementary education, which were compulsory. In Illich's view, schooling in Puerto Rico compounded matters further because those children would interiorize a sense of guilt for not having made it. Schools, then, he concluded years later, as designed, meant that the system inevitably

---

92 Everett Reimer, "Social Report. Committee on Human Resources," in Everett Reimer, *Social Planning: Collected Papers, 1957–1968*, CIDOC *Cuadernos*, no. 22 (Cuernavaca, Mexico: CIDOC, 1968 [1961]).

93 Reimer, "Social Report," 4/15.

94 Reimer, "Social Report," 4/25.

95 Ivan Illich, *Deschooling Society* (New York: Harper and Row, 1972), xix.

96 Cayley, *Rivers North of the Future*, 140.

Figure 1.1. "Together We Were Unstoppable," sculpture by Ana Jofre, 2012.
Ceramics, 24"H x 24"D x 24"W.

This piece was inspired by Aristophanes's speech on love in Plato's *Symposium*. It is a sphere with two faces and two pairs of hands and feet.

produced more dropouts than successes.[97] Cayley said that Illich began to look through the lenses of ecclesiology and liturgy at the church as an institution and its rituals and saw the school as a kind of secular church. Illich said in the conversation with Cayley decades later that he increasingly saw schooling "as the ritual of a society committed to progress and development, creating certain myths which are a requirement for a consumer society."[98] However, his writings until 1968 and his critiques were first concentrated on resignifying the role of the missionary, and between 1964 and 1968, on critiquing the church as an institution until his conflict with the Vatican.

Bishop McManus asked Illich to leave the island in 1960. Illich had strongly opposed the meddling of the local Catholic hierarchy in the election that year. The two Irish Catholic bishops had threatened to excommunicate anybody who would vote for a party that wouldn't proscribe the sale of condoms. With the help of the nuncio, the bishops had sponsored the creation of a Christian Democratic-like party.[99] Illich considered it unsound to mix religious issues with politics, a position that he would fully develop in the second part of the 1960s in relation to the Catholic hierarchy and US development planning in Latin America, in particular the Alliance for Progress. Education and the missionaries would be in the mix.

There are unanswered questions regarding his stance in relation to the institutional church. As we read in the note to the "Vanishing Clergyman," published in *Celebration of Awareness* in 1971, Illich wrote this critical text in Puerto Rico in 1959. He got a great deal of cooperation from the institutional church to put together the centres to prepare missionaries in Cuernavaca, Mexico, and it was only in 1967 that he published the first version of "The Vanishing Clergyman" in *The Critic* of Chicago.[100] Illich's experience with Puerto Ricans in New York, his work in Puerto Rico in the Intercultural Institute, and the intellectual exchanges he built there are fundamental to understanding his complex trajectory and how he reached the point of writing *Deschooling Society*.

---

97   Cayley, "Part Moon," 5.
98   Cayley, "Part Moon," 5.
99   Cayley, "Part Moon," 5.
100 Illich, "The Vanishing Clergyman." First publication, Ivan Illich, "The Vanishing Clergyman," *The Critic* 25 (June–July 1967): 18–25.

2 Beyond a Unilinear Development of Illich's Thinking: An Inquiry into Temporal Layers of Thought Forming His Critical View of the Church and the School[1]

The Political Context Framing the Creation of the Centres in Cuernavaca

Once more, we will follow the "plot" configuring Illich's thinking and political praxis. We will place Illich interacting across overlapping local (Cuernavaca, Mexico), regional (Latin America), and supranational (the US church hierarchy, the Vatican) configurations of ideas and positionings populating Latin America. We understand configurations as "spaces taken up by constellations of ideas and historical phenomena."[2] We also place Illich as an actor in relation to the actual church's structures of power. He was a leading force in the hub for ideas that his network of centres became in Cuernavaca, Mexico. As a temporal historical framework, the period of the "long 1960s" – late 1950s to mid-1970s – framing this book signalled a shift to new conceptions of education and social transformation and to challenging ways of thinking about democratic pedagogies emerging from lived experiences and revolutionary discourse and practices in Latin America.[3] The Vatican II Council (1962–5) had a great impact aimed at an *aggiornamento* of the church doctrines and practices and generated a paradigmatic shift that had been in the making outside the Vatican walls.[4]

---

1 The approach was inspired by Reinhart Koselleck, *Futures Past: On the Semantics of Historical Time* (New York: Columbia University Press, 2004).
2 Rosa Bruno-Jofré, "Localizing Dewey's Notions of Democracy and Education: A Journey Across Configurations in Latin America," *Journal of the History of Ideas* 80, no. 3 (July 2019): 433–53, quotation on 434.
3 Bruno-Jofré, "Localizing Dewey's Notions," 433.
4 Gregory Baum, "Vatican Council II: A Turning Point in the Church's History," in *Vatican II: Expériences canadiennes – Canadian Experiences*, ed. Gilles Routhier, Michael

Let's walk in the complex labyrinth of Illich's insights and the world he construed.

After returning to New York, in light of the church's need to train missionaries for Latin America, Illich made a proposal to John Considine, the head of the National Catholic Welfare Conference's Latin American Bureau (LAB), for a training program affiliated with a university in some place in Latin America.[5] In 1960 the Centre for Intercultural Formation (CIF) (1960–7) was created with offices at Fordham University, with Rev. Father Vincent O'Keefe, S.J., as its resident; Ivan Illich was appointed as CIF's executive director.[6] Illich was a priest in the diocese of New York and had been released from his duties by Cardinal Francis Spellman to serve as a professor at Fordham University. He was then released to serve as the executive director of CIF. The location at Fordham was thus a natural development, given that Illich was a faculty member there, as was his friend Joseph Fitzpatrick, S.J. Illich expected to have control over the training of the missionaries and had developed his own approach, summarized in the notion of "missionary poverty." CIF controlled all the operational budgets, and it linked the centres to ecclesiastical structures and consulting bodies such as CELAM. There were two actual formative centres. The Centre for Cultural Research (Centro de Investigaciones Culturales, CIC, 1961–6) was located eighty kilometres from Mexico City in Cuernavaca, in the former Hotel Chulavista, and served as a residence for prospective Catholic missionaries, including lay people.[7] This would be Illich's place of residence. The other, the Centre for Cultural Research (Centro de Formación Intercultural, CENFI), also a residence for missionaries, was placed in Anápolis, Brazil, at the end of 1960 but moved to Petrópolis in 1962 and closed in 1966. CENFI supervised the programs in Brazil. CENFI had its own approach, with more emphasis on social justice under the influence of Dom Hélder Câmara. In 1963 the Centre for Intercultural Documentation (Centro Intercultural de Documentación, CIDOC, 1963–76) was started within the CIC.

Attridge, and Catherine E. Clifford (Ottawa: Presses de l'Université d'Ottawa/ University of Ottawa Press, 2011), 360–77.

5   Hartch, *The Prophet of Cuernavaca*, 21.
6   "Historia del CIF, 1960–65" (Cuernavaca, Mexico: CENFI), Daniel Cosío Villegas Library, El Colegio de México, Inventario 2007, folder 370.196C397c.
7   "Requests for Funds, Center for Intercultural Documentation," 1–2, Cuernavaca, Mexico, manuscript, Biblioteca Daniel Cosío Villegas, El Colegio de México, Inventario 2007, folder 370.196C397d.

The creation of the centres was fully supported by the Latin American Bureau of the National Catholic Welfare Council (NCWC), directed by Maryknoll John Considine, who was one of the architects of the Vatican's policies. The Bureau, with funds from the NCWC, provided Illich with $75,000 to initiate the project.[8] It also financed the *CIF Reports* as well as the books and pamphlets produced by the CIC, which were used for the research in this chapter.[9] It is obvious that Illich was not initially against the papal projects and that the two centres were an integral part of Cardinal Cushing and Considine's initiatives for Latin America until 1964. It is interesting to note at this point that the CIC and CENFI were described as two well-equipped houses of the CIF, able to provide a residence and courses to prepare missionaries.

A statement in a CIF document reveals the CIF's approach to Indigenous spirituality and to coloniality in the age of "modernization" as conceived by the US sponsors. It acknowledges that many areas in Latin America were largely or completely "Indian." The text speaks for itself: "Here the Catholic from the United States will find an intermingling of Catholic practices and Indian rites and customs which is still a puzzle to many an experienced missioner and which is still being slowly unraveled by the anthropologists. It appears evident now that, although the Spanish colonizers made the Indians Catholic, they never penetrated into the mind and soul of the Indian. This is the challenge which the missioner, whether religious or lay, still faces."[10]

However, Illich had a strong critical view of the role played by missionaries in Latin America, a view he reinforced during the trip – a sort of pilgrimage – that he undertook when he returned from Puerto Rico. His goal was to put into practice his spiritual approach to mission and missionary based on his notion of the church's apostles as announcers of the gospel and as inspired by the Pauline epistles. His was a

---

8 Matthew John O'Meagher, "Catholicism, Reform, and Development in Latin America, 1959–67" (PhD diss., Department of History, Duke University 1994), 377. An annual investment of $173,500 was budgeted for the CIF and the two centres.

9 The complete collection of the *CIF Reports: Cultures, The Church, The Americas* was compiled in six volumes and published by the Intercultural Centre for Documentation (CIDOC) in 1969 and 1970 under the series *CIDOC Cuadernos*, nos. 36, 37, 38, 39, 40, and 41. The pamphlets related to the centres of Cuernavaca and Petrópolis were found in folder 370.196C397d, at the Daniel Cossío Villegas Library, El Colegio de México (Mexico DF). The *CIDOC Dossiers, Fuentes para el Estudio de las Ideologías en el Cambio Social de América Latina* are publications created by the CIDOC of Cuernavaca.

10 "Lay Apostles to Latin America: Problem or Promise," Daniel Cossío Villegas Library, El Colegio de México, folder 370.196C397d.

profoundly spiritual notion of a universal church that contrasted with the political role that the official line of the church was playing in the missions. It brought a new ethical approach grounded in the notion of the church conceived as She and inspired by the spirit, while the papal programs understood the missions as "ecclesiocentric" – as responding to the needs of the church as It, as institution. In 1961 he started to receive missionaries from PAVLA (Papal Volunteers for Latin America) and from the religious congregations.

To understand Illich's political maneuvering, here we take into account his inside understanding of the bureaucracy of the Vatican (he was immersed there during his formation), as well as the way the various institutions of the church operated, the experience he acquired in Puerto Rico, and his critical views of the institutionalized church. We are keeping in mind that he drafted "The Vanishing Clergyman" in Puerto Rico. It is not easy to infer his intentionality and how he saw both the use of a means to an end and how to relate to his Thomistic framework.

Illich inserted himself within the configuration that embodied the institutional response of the Catholic Church to what the hierarchy perceived as major threats: the expansion of Protestantism and the impact of the Cuban Revolution (1953–9), the grassroots victory in Latin America, and social unrest in Latin America. The Vatican and the US church, with Canadian participation, would converge with US policies for Latin America. What was the positioning of the Vatican and the institutional North American church? How did Latin American bishops place themselves in relation to church planning?

We need to go back to the creation of the Episcopal Latin American Conference (CELAM) in 1955 to understand that Latin American bishops were not necessarily in tune with the hierarchy from the north or even the Vatican and that they generated their own fields of meanings and institutional frameworks.[11] CELAM was created during the International Eucharistic Congress in Rio de Janeiro in 1955. This unprecedented meeting was called by the Holy See and presided over by a cardinal on behalf of the pope; notably, the Vatican revised the conclusions before publication. The topics of the meeting included the lack of priests, religious instruction, social problems, and Indigenous issues. CELAM was composed of representatives from national

---

11 We discuss this in Rosa Bruno-Jofré and Jon Igelmo Zaldívar, "The Center for
    Intercultural Formation, Cuernavaca, Mexico, Its Reports (1962–1967) and Illich's
    Critical Understanding of Mission in Latin America," *Hispania Sacra* LXV, Extra II
    (July–December 2013): 7–31.

episcopal conferences whose mandate was to discuss current issues, promote and support Catholic work with communities, and organize Episcopal Latin American conferences called by the Holy See.[12] It was the Vatican's centralized approach. A framework of mutual missionary help had already emerged from Pius XII's encyclical *Fidei Donum*, published in April 1957,[13] encouraging cooperation between the dioceses of ancient traditions and regions of more recent evangelization – having Africa in mind, but within the context of the needs of the church.[14] For example, within this framework, the diocese of St. Boniface, Manitoba, Canada, sent a team of priests and sisters to work in Brazil.[15] Pius XII created in 1958 the Pontifical Commission for Latin America.

The Holy See with John XXIII moved towards the goal of building a Catholic Inter-American Cooperation Program (CICOP) on its own terms, in a pan-American approach. Thus, John XXIII asked Archbishop Antonio Samoré – who had organized the 1955 Eucharistic Congress in Rio from which CELAM developed – to be in charge of Latin American issues. The archbishop played a role in the organization of the First Inter-American Conference held between 2 and 4 November 1959 at the School of Linguistics at Georgetown University; it was convoked by the Pontifical Commission for Latin America and presided over by Cardinal Richard Cushing of Boston. There were, upfront, three problems to be addressed in Latin America: a shortage of clergy, the advances of communism, and the expansion of Protestantism. There were eighteen bishops, six each from Canada, the United States, and Latin America, who worked with a question posed by Samoré: "What was the U.S. church prepared to do for its brothers and sisters in the south?"[16]

---

12 François Houtart, "L'Histoire du CELAM ou l'oubli des origines" [The History of CELAM or the Forgotten Origins], *Archives de sciences sociales des religions* 62, no. 1 (July–September 1986): 93–105.

13 Pius XII, *Fidei Donum*, Encyclical on the Present Condition of the Catholic Missions, Especially in Africa (Vatican: The Holy See, 21 April 1957), http://w2.vatican.va /content/pius-xii/en/encyclicals/documents/hf_p-xii_enc_21041957_fidei -donum.html.

14 Father Edouard Banville, "Missionary Experience in Brazil 1960–1980," interview and translation by Sister Dora Tétreault, Missionary Oblate Sister, Winnipeg, Manitoba, 16 and 20 August 2013, located in the Archives of the Missionary Oblate Sisters, AMO, Winnipeg.

15 Rosa Bruno-Jofré, "Encountering Social Change at a Time of Rapid Radicalization of the National Church: The Missionary Oblate Sisters in Brazil," *Historical Studies (Canadian Catholic Historical Association)* 85 (2019): 57–72.

16 Antonio Samoré, quoted in James F. Garneau, "The First Inter-American Episcopal Conference, November 2–4, 1959: Canada and the United States Called to the Rescue of Latin America," in *The Catholic Historical Review* 87, no. 4 (2001): 662.

The official objective was to build a pan-American collaboration and strengthen the church in Latin America. It was a broad approach to missionary work with strong political implications, rather than joint support for one specific project. Cardinal Richard Cushing advocated the promotion of the social doctrine of the church and social reforms to counter communism.[17] He considered communism to be the greatest enemy of the church.

Meanwhile, Bishop Manuel Larraín from Chile and Dom Hélder Câmara, at the time (1959) auxiliary bishop of Rio de Janeiro, had a different vision for Latin America even as they were part of the hierarchy. Câmara said at the meeting that "the egotism of many rich people, their blindness, is a more serious and urgent problem than communism itself."[18] Câmara, who would help Ivan Illich to organize the centre in Petrópolis, also said, "the task ahead of us is not to mobilize alms. Our first objective is to lead public opinion to understand that raising the under-developed world is a much more serious and urgent problem than the East-West conflict itself."[19] This would be the best way to defeat communism. In response to Cushing, he made clear the need for "consciousness" on the part of one-third of humanity – who were capable of helping and thus obliged to assist – of the "misery and hunger" of two thirds of humanity, in order to re-establish human dignity. In Câmara's view, this misery was more serious than communism. Cushing replied by offering 25,000 copies of FBI Director J. Edgar Hoover's book *Masters of Deceit*,[20] and his own book, *Questions and Answers on Communism*, which he reported had been "checked by the F. B. I.," as well as films on the mysteries of the rosary produced by Father Patrick J. Peyton.[21] Both Cushing and Hoover were obsessed with communism within the framework of the Cold War.

A number of bishops in Latin America had taken a regional approach to dealing with poverty and injustice, and they encouraged the people's participation, often, particularly in the late 1950s, in the form of popular developmentalism. There were, for example, popular education

---

17 Cardinal Richard Cushing, *Questions et réponses sur le communisme* (Sherbrooke, Montréal, Paris: Apostolat de la Presse, 1961), 49.
18 Willard F. Barber, "Can the Alliance for Progress Succeed?" *Annals of the American Academy of Political and Social Science* 351, no. 1 (1964): 89.
19 Hélder Câmara, quoted in Garneau, "The First Inter-American Episcopal Conference," 680; see also Hélder Câmara, *Revolution through Peace* (New York: Colophon Books, 1972).
20 J. Edgar Hoover, *Master of Deceit: The Story of Communism in America and How to Fight It* (New York: Henry Holt and Company, 1958).
21 Garneau, "The First Inter-American Episcopal Conference," 681.

initiatives sponsored by the Northeast church in Brazil in the 1950s, such as the Natal Movement and the Movimiento de Educación de Base (Grassroots Education Movement, or MEB).[22] The MEB was described by Marina Bandeira later in 1964 "as a supporter of necessary change, of the total participation of workers in things that concern them; it is not just a new campaign against illiteracy; we fight the conditions producing it."[23] The Brazilian Bishops had their own regional Episcopal conferences in the 1950s.[24] The *CIF Report* recorded that the General Assembly of Brazilian Bishops had produced an "Emergency Plan" or "Plan of Urgency" that addressed pastoral issues as well as directives in relation to the socio-economic dimension of MEB, and in relation to the agrarian leagues (oriented towards rural unions) and eventual collaboration with the Alliance for Progress.[25]

There was also a process of convergence of Christianity and Marxism by "selected affinity."[26] Michael Löwy made the point that the Brazilian Christian left of the early 1960s – in the form of Juventude Universitária Cristã (Christian Academic Youth, or JUC), Juventude Estudantil Cristã (Christian Student Youth, or JEC), and Açao Popular (Popular Action, or AP) – "was the first manifestation in Latin America of the articulation between Christian faith and Marxist politics as a movement with a broad social base, in academia and even among the clergy."[27] This process, Löwy asserts, began before Vatican II, the comunidades eclesiales de base (grassroots communities), liberation theology, and the 1964 military coup.[28] Brazil was one of those scenarios where there was a rapid process of radicalization and counterattack by the right. Hélder Câmara embodied an ebullient social setting where the Catholic Church was a strong protagonist, and he was not alone. Interestingly, when in August

---

22 See also Andrew Dawson, "A Very Brazilian Experiment: The Base Education Movement 1961–67," *History of Education* 31, no. 2 (2002): 185–94.

23 Marina Bandeira, "MEB – 'Movimento de Educação de Base,'" report given to the Catholic Inter-American Cooperation Program (CICOP), Chicago, 23 January 1964, compiled in *CIF Reports*, vol. 3, April–December 1964: 1/12, *CIDOC Cuaderno*, no. 38 (Cuernavaca, Mexico: CIDOC, 1970).

24 Scott Mainwaring, *The Catholic Church and Politics in Brazil, 1916–1985* (Stanford, CA: Stanford University Press, 1986), 94.

25 General Assembly of Brazilian Bishops, 1963, "Brazilian Bishops' Emergency Plan," reproduced from Perspectives de Catholicité XXIIe, Année, 1963, no. 4, compiled in *CIF Reports*, vol. 3, April–December 1964: 1/10, *CIDOC Cuaderno*, no. 38 (Cuernavaca, Mexico: CIDOC, 1970).

26 Michael Löwy, translated by Claudia Pompan, "Marxism and Christianity in Latin America," *Latin American Perspectives* 20, no. 4 (1993): 32.

27 Löwy, "Marxism and Christianity," 32.

28 Löwy, "Marxism and Christianity," 33.

1961, two Canadian priests took charge of the first parish in the French quarter in the north of São Paulo, Santa Joanna d'Arch (Jeanne d'Arc), an industrial area with 35,000 inhabitants, the mass was already in Portuguese.[29] Already in 1960 ideas about grassroots Christian communities were spreading, and people had gathered to form communities; the parishes would become networks of small communities of twenty to thirty people each. Leonard Boff, a Franciscan, and a young Dominican, Carlos Maesters, were spearheading this development. The coup d'état of 1964 put an end to the peasant and labour movements. In the scheme of things, the church in Latin America can be understood as a field (making use of Bourdieu here), with not only different positionings and configurations of political ideas, but also structural contradictions.[30] We need to add to this the emergence of liberation theology that provided an orientation to the grassroots movement and that would inspire various expressions of popular education all over Latin America into the very early 1980s.

The official line of the church politically converged with US foreign policy towards Latin America, an issue Illich would denounce later in "The Seamy Side of Charity" in 1967. It is interesting to note that the Alliance for Progress was launched on 17 August 1961 in Punta del Este, Uruguay; this was a ten-year development plan that included the modernizing vision of the Kennedy administration to deal with the "communist threat" to the region in the aftermath of the Cuban Revolution of 1959.[31] On the same day, at the University of Notre Dame, Monsignor Agostino Casaroli read on behalf of the pope the document "Appeal of the Pontifical Commission to North American Superiors," calling congregations and religious provinces to send, over a ten-year period, 10 per cent of their membership as of 1961 on missions to Latin America.[32]

29 Rosa Bruno-Jofré, "Encountering Social Change."
30 We are using here Pierre Bourdieu's notion of field. See Pierre Bourdieu, *Language and Symbolic Power*, ed. John B. Thompson, trans. Gino Raymond and Matthew Adamson (Cambridge, MA: Harvard University Press, 1993).
31 Inter-American Economic and Social Council, 1961, "The Charter of Punta Del Este: Alliance for Progress: Official Documents," in Jeffrey Taffet, *Foreign Aid as Foreign Policy: The Alliance for Progress in Latin America* (New York: Routledge, 2007), appendix at 205–23; Mark T. Berger, "'Toward Our Common American Destiny': Hemispheric History and Pan American Politics in the Twentieth Century," *Journal of Iberian and Latin American Research* 8, no. 1 (2002): 57–88; Edwin McCammon Martin, *Kennedy and Latin America* (Lanham, New York, London: University Press of America, 1994).
32 Agostini Casaroli, "Appeal of the Pontifical Commission to North American Superiors," in *Mission to Latin America: The Successes and Failures of a*

The Alliance for Progress had the Peace Corps as a strategic resource to reach Latin Americans, while the Vatican had created the Papal Volunteers in 1960. On 15 May 1961, a few months before the August call, Pope John XXIII had issued the encyclical *Mater et Magistra*,[33] which addressed social issues in light of the Catholic social doctrine, was infused with the idea of progress, differentiated between developed and underdeveloped countries and those on the way to development, as Harry Truman did,[34] and talked about inequality among individuals and nations and the need for an adequate agrarian policy based on redistribution of land.[35] The pattern of a language of reform in both *Mater et Magistra* and the Charter of the Alliance is similar. This is not surprising because within the context of hybrid approaches and processes of increasing radicalization, the church had participated in the 1950s in development projects; an example was the creation of SUDENE in 1956 as a result of the alliance between the bishops of Northeastern Brazil and President Juscelino Kubitschek, an example of cooperation between church and state through a democratic government. In 1959 Rome had exhorted the governments and the Catholic population to cooperate in developmentalist projects.[36]

There was a range of theological changes in the church outside the Vatican in the 1950s and 1960s that would reach and take their own shape in Latin America, changes that of course would have a presence at the Vatican II Council. These comprised the internationalization in the 1950s of the *nouvelle théologie* and the dissemination of the work of French Dominican priest Yves Congar, French Jesuit Henri de Lubac, and German Jesuit Karl Rahner, who opened up new avenues in social Catholicism, elaborated on a theology in which the church was engaged with the modern world, and were critical of the social functions of the church. It was a time of great diffusion of the work of Jacques Maritain

---

   Twentieth-Century Crusade, ed. Gerald M. Costello (New York: Orbis Books, 1979), appendix at 273–81.

33 John XXIII, *Mater et Magistra*, Encyclical on Christianity and Social Progress (Vatican: Holy See, 15 May 1961), http://www.vatican.va/content/john-xxiii/en /encyclicals/documents/hf_j-xxiii_enc_15051961_mater.html.

34 Wolfgang Sachs, *The Development Dictionary: A Guide to Knowledge as Power* (New York: Zed Books, 1992).

35 J. Comblin, "La Iglesia latinoamericana desde el Vaticano II," *Documentación Política* No. 7, Contacto X, año 15, 1 (February), (Agence Latino-Américaine d'Information [ALAI], Centre de Documentation d'Amérique Latine- SUCO, 1978), 119–24.

36 Antonio Samoré, quoted in James F. Garneau, "The First Inter-American Episcopal Conference, November 2–4, 1959: Canada and the United States Called to the Rescue of Latin America," *The Catholic Historical Review* 87, no. 4 (2001): 662.

and Étienne Gilson and their humanism. During this period a number of priests came back to Latin America after their formative years in Europe, in particular in Louvain. Social Catholicism had taken on a new configuration, as conveyed in the programs in Latin America and in the development of the Christian Democratic Parties. Vatican II opened the church to the modern world, but Vatican II documents were read in Latin America through the people's experience and their historical reality. This opened a window that legitimized a theological thinking rooted in the suffering of the people that would take shape in liberation theology. Many congregations lived the radicality of the gospel.

The complacent relationship that foreign missionaries, in particular Americans, had cultivated between a benevolent United States and Latin America after the Second World War had been shaken. Missionaries recognized this. The Maryknolls, for example, in the 1960s, distanced their mission from the United States, while living the values of what appeared to be an emergent Catholic Church responding to Vatican II, as well as to the advent of liberation theology, social movements in the United States, and a new generation of missionaries. The emphasis moved away from economic aid from the north.[37] Furthermore, the Cuban Revolution in 1959, with its grassroots character, had generated great sympathy in Latin America, and the Cold War rhetoric acquired a new discursive component.[38]

The 1960s and early 1970s were characterized by a political landscape that quickly moved towards radicalization, threatening American interests. The response was given through a series of coups d'état that brought the military to power: in Brazil in 1964, Bolivia in 1964, Panamá in 1968, Uruguay in 1973, Chile in 1973, and Argentina in 1976. The establishment of repressive states went along with neoliberal market policies.

Cuernavaca, a Refractive Micro-Cosmos

Illich hovered over and worked out his agenda to prepare missionaries, whose role he resignified with a spiritual re-orientation. He selected Cuernavaca as the site for the formative centre for missionaries. It was there that he had met Bishop Sergio Méndez Arceo, who

---

37 Susan Fitzpatrick-Behrens, *The Maryknoll Catholic Mission in Peru, 1943–1989* (Notre Dame, IN: University of Notre Dame Press, 2012), 152–3.
38 Thomas C. Field Jr., Stella Krepp, and Vani Pettinà, *Latin America and the Global Cold War* (London: University College, 2020).

had a transformative vision of the role of the church. Illich's writings and work need to be read in relation to his past, his formation, the Latin American context, the structure of the church, and particularly the context in Cuernavaca and the people with whom he interacted. A particular configuration of ideas emerged there, with psychoanalysis having an important place in that configuration. Cuernavaca was an experimental micro-cosmos with powerful transformative characters in interaction with a very conservative Mexican Catholic hierarchy associated with the powerful, who were preserving its structure of power. We cannot neglect the centre in Anápolis that moved to Petrópolis or the powerful presence of Hélder Câmara, as we will see.

The church there, under the leadership of the bishop, had begun a liturgical, aesthetic, social, and cultural *aggiornamento* before the Second Vatical Council (1962–5). In the late 1950s Bishop Sergio Méndez Arceo renovated the Cathedral, one of the oldest in Mexico, stripping out the Baroque altar and the nineteenth-century ornaments and removing all the statues of saints, leaving only the statue of the Virgin Mary. The interior of the Cathedral was restored to show the early Franciscan missionary style, with the stone slab serving as the altar dominated by a bronze ciborium flanked by bronze lecterns and a filiform wooden cross.[39] The newly uncovered coarse walls revealed original seventeenth-century depictions of the martyrdom of St. Philip, the missionary priest and Mexican Saint.[40] This was in line with Méndez Arceo's democratic and humble style and his criticism of a church that was reverent to civil authority for its own material interests, while its messianic role was to serve as a constant critic of secular power.[41]

Méndez Arceo, a bishop who trusted in the Holy Spirit and felt comfortable with a Pentecostal atmosphere, of course had to manage the opposition of the conservative Mexican church, which would also be uncomfortable with the mariachi band in the Mass and the distribution of Bibles in Spanish. His church positions were different from the official position of the church and from that of Considine, who, as we said before, was the architect of the Catholic plan for Latin America and had

---

39 Francine du Plessix Gray, *Divine Disobedience: Profiles in Catholic Radicalism* (New York: Alfred A. Knopf, 1970), 259–60. See also B. López (comp.), *Cuernavaca: Fuentes para el Estudio de la Diócesis, CIDOC Dossier*, xxxi, ii (Cuernavaca, Mexico: CIDOC, 1968), 4/468–5/16; María del Carmen Turrent, "El sentido de los murales de la Catedral de Cuernavaca," *Inventio* iii (2006): 5–10.

40 du Plessix Gray, *Divine Disobedience*, 260.

41 du Plessix Gray, *Divine Disobedience*, 260.

Figure 2.1. Sergio Méndez Arceo Cuernavaca, bishop of Cuernavaca, exiting his cathedral in 1970.

Source: Licensed under the Creative Commons Attribution-Share Alike 3.0 Unported license (https://creativecommons.org/licenses/by-sa/3.0/deed.en), available at https://commons.wikimedia.org/wiki/File:Sergio_Mendez_Arceo_bishop_Cuernavaca_1970.jpg.

the ear of the pope. The Latin American Bureau headed by Considine was fully aligned with Cardinal Richard Cushing of Boston, a personal friend of the Kennedys and a staunch anti-communist who was committed to the Alliance for Progress and who engaged with the discourse of the Cold War.[42]

Cuernavaca had moved towards a social and cultural *aggiornamento* even before the publication of decrees and documents from Vatican II (1962–5), and also towards an *aggiornamento* with developments in the social sciences and in psychology, in particular with the place of psychoanalysis in religious life. Méndez Arceo actually approved in 1961 the use of psychoanalysis by the Benedictine monastery of Santa María de la Resurrección, near Cuernavaca, whose prior was Gregorio Lemercier. Illich had a close relationship with Lemercier;[43] he had been

---

42 Garneau, "The First Inter-American Episcopal Conference."
43 Lya Gutiérrez Quintanilla, *Los Volcanes de Cuernavaca: Sergio Méndez Arceo, Gregorio Lemercier, Ivan Illich* (Morelos, Mexico: La Jornada, 2007); du Plessix Gray, *Divine Disobedience*, 271.

in Cuernavaca since 1951, the same year Méndez Arceo had arrived in the city, and they had become close friends. Lemercier's community began to sing Mass in the Spanish vernacular the same year and discarded the Latin liturgy. It has been argued that his avant-gardism was a major influence on Méndez Arceo's engagement with modernity, as he had been quite moderate in his views.[44] The monastery was involved in social services, including food distribution to the poor and health services, and the monks helped those experiencing illness of the soul, worked in their workshops and on their farm, and participated in struggles for social justice alongside Méndez Arceo.[45]

The experience with the external world raised questions among the members of the monastery. Former monk Alejandro Chao Barona recalled later that many of the monks were not in a good mental state and that their demons were not external but were the monks' own demons, passions, strivings, and searches.[46] Prior Lemercier went through rigorous psychoanalytical therapy with Gustavo Quevedo after suffering a hallucination in October 1960. In June 1961 the prior extended the therapy to the members of the monastery, who became involved in group therapy. One of the therapists was Argentinian Fryda Zmud.[47] Alejandro Chao Barona described the experience as illuminating: "all this psychoanalytical work was really conscientization, what we were looking for was a clear consciousness of our spirituality within the search for spirituality itself."[48] The order to stop the provision of psychoanalytical therapy came from the Vatican, and in 1965 it began proceedings against the monastery, which was then closed in 1967.[49] Lemercier had strong opposition from the conservative Mexican clergy. While dealing with the dispute over psychotherapy, the monastery kept in touch not only with Méndez Arceo, who was very close to Lemercier, but with Ivan Illich and his centres.

Another major figure who was living in Cuernavaca and who would become a neighbour and close friend of Illich was Erich Fromm, the social psychoanalyst, who also tried to help the monastery in its

44 du Plessix Gray, *Divine Disobedience*, 261; Gutiérrez Quintanilla, *Los Volcanes de Cuernavaca*.

45 Gutiérrez Quintanilla, *Los Volcanes de Cuernavaca*, 65.

46 Gutiérrez Quintanilla, *Los Volcanes de Cuernavaca*, 66.

47 J.A. Litmanovich, "Las Operaciones Psicoanalíticas gestadas al interior del monasterio Benedictino de Ahuacatlitlán, Cuernavaca, Morelos, Mexico (1961–1964)" (unpublished PhD diss., Universidad Iberoameticana de Mexico, 2008).

48 Gutiérrez Quintanilla, *Los Volcanes de Cuernavaca*, 66.

49 Henry Giniger, "A Monastery in Mexico Closed in Dispute Over Psychoanalysis," *New York Times*, 6 September 1967, 15.

Figure 2.2. Catedral de la Ciudad de Cuernavaca, Morelos, by José Luis Tristan Espino.

Source: Licensed under the Creative Commons Attribution-Share Alike 3.0 Unported license (https://creativecommons.org/licenses/by-sa/3.0/deed.en), available at https://es.wikipedia.org/wiki/Catedral_de_Cuernavaca#/media/Archivo:02564 _COPIA_CATEDRAL_CUERNAVACA.jpg.

spiritual search and links to the psychological.[50] Fromm wrote introductions to Illich's work and contributed to *CIDOC Informa*.[51] He had been involved with the Institute for Social Research, known as the

---

50 Lawrence J. Friedman, assisted by Anke M. Schreiber, *The Lives of Erich Fromm: Love's Prophet* (New York: Columbia University Press, 2013), 294.
51 *CIDOC Informa* was published between April 1964 and June 1970. Initially, it reproduced the same material as in the *CIF Reports*, but in their original language

Frankfurt School, that opened in Frankfurt, Germany, in 1924. It was a neo-Marxist institute that elaborated a critique of capitalism; its leading thinkers were philosophers Max Horkheimer, Theodor Adorno, and Herbert Marcuse, and social psychoanalyst Erich Fromm, among others, while philosopher Walter Benjamin had a close relationship to the institute.[52] The most recent phase of the Frankfurt School had moved away from Marxism under the influence of Jürgen Habermas. Fromm and others were involved, particularly from the 1930s, in the use of psychoanalytic theory to explain the capitalist consumerism of the working classes and the reasons for their attraction to Nazism. Fromm was part of Illich's team and also close to Lemercier and Méndez Arceo. Fromm questioned the frame of Freud's original theories, in particular the mechanistic materialism dominant among natural scientists at the beginning of the twentieth century. He claimed that further development of Freud's thought required dialectical humanism as a frame of reference; by opening up Freud's discoveries, such as the Oedipus complex, narcissism, and the death instinct, and by framing them within humanism, they would become more meaningful.[53]

Psychoanalysis occupied a central place in the intellectual life of the time in Latin America and in Cuernavaca. Méndez Arceo, convinced that psychoanalysis could be used to "purify vocations,"[54] invited Lemercier to go with him to Rome in September 1965, during the fourth period of the Vatican II Council, when Schema 13 on the church and the modern world was being discussed. Méndez Arceo made an unsuccessful appeal for psychoanalysis and argued on behalf of ten Latin American bishops that it was as important as the work of Darwin and Galileo. In his view, the Council was taking a sociological approach in the discussion of Schema 13, while disregarding the anthropological perspective. In Arceo's mind, modern human beings were more self-aware and self-conscious, more associable, and tended to rationalize

---

(Spanish). It also published documents that were used in the preparation of the *CIF Reports*.

52 Stuart Jeffries, *Grand Hotel Abyss: The Lives of the Frankfurt School* (London and New York: Verso, 2017).

53 Erich Fromm, *The Heart of Man: Its Genius for Good and Evil* (New York, 1964). This is also a similar paragraph to that published in Rosa Bruno-Jofré and Jon Igelmo Zaldívar, "Monsignor Ivan Illich's Critique of the Institutional Church, 1960–1966," *Journal of Ecclesiastical History* 65, no. 3 (July 2016): 568–86, quotation on 575.

54 Sergio Méndez Arceo, "Intervención Conciliar, Algunas Observaciones al Esquema XIII," in López, Fuentes para el Estudio de una Diocesis, 1, 4/154–8. The full text of Méndez Arceo's presentation is reproduced in Latin as it was written.

their position vis-à-vis the Absolute. This positioning in relation to the Absolute often led, in his view, to atheism, as with psychoanalysis human beings become aware of themselves. For Arceo, "psychoanalysis is irreversibly in the discourse of the humane. It is a true science in the modern sense." He went on to say that "with psychoanalysis, human beings do not move to mistrust but to dialogue."[55] The preoccupation with neurotic personalities and affective problems among religious and the use of psychoanalysis was quite extensive, and this was not unique to Cuernavaca.[56]

Illich skilfully interacted within an opposing set of interests and views. He was inserted in the conservative configuration of the church and its structures, using its services and financing, while opening up a new conception of missionary work grounded in his theological vision of the gospel and the apostles. At the same time, the micro-cosmos of Cuernavaca, which embodied the global currents of ideas of the day while being inserted defiantly in a conservative setting, further cultivated Illich's critique of processes of institutionalization and the institutionalization of the church.

Illich's Conception of the Missionary

At the core, there were contesting intentionalities in relation to the formation of the missionary that made sense within the context of the objectives and politics of the official church vis-à-vis the theological influences and Illich's experience in New York and Puerto Rico and his early questioning of institutionalization. Particularly relevant was Illich's notion of poverty, central to the missionary formation that he fully embraced when working with Puerto Ricans and forming priests to work with Puerto Ricans. Illich's resignification was grounded in his notion of the church's apostles as announcers of the gospel and as inspired by the Pauline epistles. In this early vision of the missionary role, missionaries were to incarnate themselves in the culture rather than becoming agents of their own culture, with "poverty" as a central

---

55 "Méndez Arceo habla al fin," in B. López, compilador, *Cuernavaca Fuentes para el Estudio de una Diócesis, CIDOC Dossier* xxxi, i (Cuernavaca, Mexico: CIDOC, 1968), 4/188–4/195, at 193. The article was reproduced from *Siempre*, Cuernavaca (27 March 1966), 8, 9. See "Mexican Bishop Endorses Freud: Ecumenical Council is Told Catholic Church Should Back Psychoanalysis," *New York Times*, 29 September 1965, 1, column 4.

56 See Luis Bravo Valdivieso (Santiago, Chile) to Monseñor Sergio Méndez Arceo (Vatican Council, Rome), 12 November 1965, in López, Fuentes para el estudio de una diócesis, ii, 4/273–4/275.

virtue.[57] Illich linked missionary "poverty" to being part of a process in which the missionary divests herself from values and assumptions to meet others where they are, "if he [sic] wants to be truly an instrument of the Incarnation rather than an agent of his [sic] own culture. No missioner has the right to insist, in the name of the Gospel, on acceptance of his [sic] own human background ... Without an understanding of this distinction between imposition and absorption of cultural patterns, the Catholic missions cannot be understood, nor the concept of cultures developed under the influence of the church and the church's own cultural cloak."[58] The missioner witnesses "the relativity of human convictions in front of the unique and absolute meaning of the Revelation."[59]

There is a mystical element in Illich's notions of love and incarnation: "love urges us to become like those we love," and the missionaries "seek to become like the people they are sent to adopt yet do not cease to be sons [sic] of their native country."[60] Love is at the core of the apostolate, he thought, and can be encapsulated in the notion of "poverty" of the missionary. Illich did not accept cultural imperialism from priests, sisters, and missionaries, nor the sense of American exceptionalism that was embedded in the papal volunteers (PAVLA). His understanding of mission would naturally lead to a critical view of the role of the missionary. Cayley wrote that the revelation in the New Testament is, according to Illich, a summons beyond cultural and religious containment: "What the Samaritan does is to step fearlessly outside what his culture has sanctified in order to create a new relationship and, potentially, a new community. He does not seek God within a sacred circle but finds him lying by the road in a ditch. His possibilities cannot be predicted or circumscribed. He lives, in the apostle Paul's words, 'not under the law, but under grace.'"[61] Still, there is in Illich's thought a notion of universality that in the end embodies an ethnocentric notion, placing the Judeo-Christian tradition and revelation in the New Testament at the centre of humanhood and the only God. This is

---

57 Ivan Illich, "The Philosophy of Intercultural Formation," in *Training for Apostolic Service in Latin America* (Centre of Intercultural Formation, Fordham, New York, Cuernavaca, Mexico, Anapolis, Brazil), pamphlet, Daniel Cosío Villegas Library, El Colegio de México, Inventario 2007, folder 370.196C397c. This version is from before 1962.

58 Illich, "The Philosophy of Intercultural Formation," folder 370.196C397c, 8–9.

59 Illich, "The Philosophy of Intercultural Formation," folder 370.196C397d, 21.

60 Centre for Intercultural Formation (CIF), "Pope John XXIII, Feast of the Annunciation," pamphlet.

61 David Cayley, *The Rivers North of the Future: The Testament of Ivan Illich as Told to David Cayley* (Toronto: House of Anansi, 2005), 31–2.

particularly relevant in terms of Latin America and its history of colonization of Indigenous peoples.

Illich understood that fluency in Spanish "to communicate fully within an Hispano-American frame of mind" was fundamental, as it was "an acquaintance with the socio-economic realities of their missionaries' surroundings."[62] There is no mention of Indigenous languages. When learning a language, in Illich's words, it is not only a matter of learning sounds but of grasping the subtleties of the meaning of silence, as silences are part of the missionary's process of divesting herself from values and assumptions to meet the other. If s/he does not realize the importance of silence in learning a language and "tries to buy the language as a suit," s/he becomes the one who forgets the analogy of the silence of God and the silence of others – "a man [sic] who tries basically to rape the culture into which he [sic] is sent ... he [sic] is away from home but has never landed anywhere, [so] that he [sic] [has] left his [sic] home and never reached another."[63] Illich wrote in another text, "The Incarnation is the infinite prototype of missionary activity, the communication of the Gospel to those who are 'other', through Him who entered a world by nature not His own. Just as the Word without ceasing to be what He is, became man, Jew, Roman subject, member of a culture at a given moment in history, so any missionary, without ever ceasing to be what he is, enters and becomes part of a 'foreign' culture as it is at the present moment in a given place."[64] Illich saw the church in line with the vision of the church "as the mystical body of Christ" that had actually been adopted by the Vatican. The mission of the church would be to continue that incarnation.

Illich's early intentionality seems imbued with the notion of the church as the mystical body of Christ, but it may have as a point of reference the differentiation that Illich had, in retrospect and as mentioned before, made between the church as It (the institution) and the church as She.[65] Another point of reference was his conception of Catholicity and of the universality of the church, which is built across difference rather than on exportation of ways of experiencing faith, hence the notion of

---

62 "Center of Intercultural Formation, 1961 Cuernavaca, Mexico; Petrópolis, Brazil; Fordham University, N.Y.C." (Cuernavaca, Mexico: CIF, 1961), manuscript, Daniel Cosío Villegas Library, El Colegio de México, Inventario 2007, folder 370.196C397d.
63 Ivan Illich, "The Eloquence of Silence," in *Celebration of Awareness: A Call for Institutional Revolution* (Garden City, NY: Doubleday, 1971), 36.
64 "Center of Intercultural Formation," 19.
65 Cayley, *Rivers North of the Future*, 4.

incarnation; it was originally a church without the pitfalls of the institutionalization of central values, such as hospitality and charity.

He was already questioning the institutionalization of human values and ways of being. We find in his discourse various layers of temporality, as he often seems to go back to the early days of the Jesus movement, a time when there was no "church" in the first generation, just gatherings (ecclesiae, meaning house gatherings), in which there were no priests and there were many charisms inspired by the Holy Spirit.[66] Illich would also often refer to medieval times, and we find elements of neo-medievalism in his negative approach to the state. His early conception of the missionary would be further complicated by the influence of psychoanalysis. Already in the 1961 statement entitled "The Philosophy of Intercultural Formation," when explaining how to become profoundly poor by seeking poverty at an intimate level, by leaving our culture and the ways we think things need to be done, he clarifies this by referring to culture as an aspect of what Freud meant by "super ego."[67]

Illich had a vision of the role of the missionaries. In his retrospective view in 1992, in conversation with Cayley, he said:

> I asked myself – not about the average bureaucratic little puppet which most of these missionaries and papal volunteers and Peace Corps people were, people who were just seeking experience, avoiding the draft, or looking for adventure – I asked, What happens when the serious, the good ones, the responsible ones, are sent to Peru, come to a village, and try to live like the people? ...
>
> Therefore, the volunteer becomes a demonstration model for high levels of service consumption when you send him [sic] to Latin America. I wanted to point out the damage, the damage done by volunteerism, the damage to the person who went there through the establishment of a sense of superiority, a savior complex, and the damage to the image in the U.S. of what poor countries are. Through volunteers this image came to be dependent not only on journalists but on people who claimed that they could report with much better knowledge of local situations – in the light of these people needing us![68]

Cayley concluded that the centres were subversive from the beginning. The actual journey was a bit nuanced along the way, although Illich,

---

66 Garry Wills, *Why Priests? A Failed Tradition* (New York: Penguin Book, 2014), 1.
67 Illich, "The Philosophy of Intercultural Formation," folder 370.196C397c, 11.
68 David Cayley, *Ivan Illich in Conversation* (Toronto: Anansi, 1992), 93–4.

with political savvy, prepared missionaries with a spiritually resignified notion of mission from the very start. We, during our research, constantly encountered as leitmotif Illich's questioning of processes of institutionalization affecting the human soul – questioning that he would later move to schooling – his distrust of modernity, and his resistance of processes of centralization that we can trace theologically to Maritain. All of these elements would appear ingrained in Illich's writings, albeit imbued by new components generated by intellectual and ideological intersections and Illich's interaction at various levels.

The Centres and Their Programs, 1961–6: Building Hubs

CIC

The Centro de Investigaciones Culturales/Centre of Cultural Research (CIC) located in Cuernavaca, at the former Hotel Chulavista, was formally registered as a non-profit Mexican civil association that delivered, twice a year, two four-month programs of formation consisting of three major components: Spanish language, spiritual formation, and skills in intercultural communication with extensive political and socio-economic components. Contradictions in the spiritual conception of the church's role and the educational goals of the centre were conveyed in the tension between Illich, who ran the centres in the field, and his friend Hélder Câmara, who was influential in CENFI, and those around them – with the church establishment personified in John Considine and the US cardinals and embodied in US policy.

CIC opened and received the first missionaries in 1960. In July 1961 the first group coming to the centre, made up of fifty people, was integrated: eight priests, twelve women religious, and thirty lay people. Of the thirty lay people, seven were members of the Association of International Development, known as AID, in reference to the US Agency for International Development (US AID) created in November 1961.[69] One third of the lay volunteers who had registered had to be advised that they were not suited to the second half of the four-month course.[70]

---

69 "Lay Apostles to Latin America: Problems or Promise," folder 370.196C397d, Daniel Cosío Villegas Library, El Colegio de México, Documento no publicado, p. 1. The Agency was created in November 1961. This is puzzling because the document refers to the first group of volunteers attending CIC; the agency included workers from other organizations that became part of AID.

70 "The CIF Puzzle," unpublished document (report of the first two months of its first course in Cuernavaca), Carpeta 370.196C397d.

Among the organizations sending volunteers to the centres in Cuernavaca and Brazil were AID, PAVLA, Grail, the Peace Corps, Misereor (Germany, Bishop's fund against Hunger and Sickness), Ad Lucem, and others.[71] We would make a side point here that we shouldn't be surprised by the presence of AID workers, given the umbrella of support to CIF that initially included of course Spellman, John Considine, and Cardinal Cushing. The agency had a strong mandate in relation to US national security and modernization. We know that in Latin America at the time people linked AID and even the Peace Corps to the CIA, and we wonder whether those who did not adapt to the problem were those indicated here as AID workers, or whether there was another concern. An early report states the need for more careful screening and that a better understanding of the training at CIF (through CIC) might have prevented the admission of non-suitable candidates.[72] The situation reveals the complexity of Illich's political praxis, aimed at reaching his goals of infusing change within Christian spirituality and questioning institutionalization and the partisan political participation of the church. Thus, as we will see, Illich would be engaged in a critical appraisal of the role of PAVLA in Latin America even as he accepted trainees in Cuernavaca and Petrópolis. At the core was his conception of the role of the missionary. The resignification of this role became embroiled with Illich's own evolution and his critique of the church, as well as his exposure to new ideas; different temporalities corresponding to layers of experiences and ways of thinking that overlapped and often intertwined characterized the life of the centres. We are referring here to neo-medievalist remnants, neo-Thomism, phenomenology, psychoanalysis, and anti-imperialist positioning.

Building the Hub in Cuernavaca

In 1963, Illich established in Cuernavaca, within CIC, the Centro Intercultural de Documentación/Centre for Intercultural Documentation (CIDOC) to provide bibliographical information on the relationship between socio-economic and church development. It requested funding in 1964, when CIF/CIC had already been engaged in various publications and received journals, magazines, and documentation from all over the world and CIDOC had opened. CIDOC would assemble all

---

71 "Lay Apostles to Latin America," 3.
72 "The C.I.F. Puzzle," Daniel Cosío Villegas Library, El Colegio de México, folder 370.196C397d. No date or signature is available; as it was written in Cuernavaca, it can be inferred that was written c. October 1961.

the documentation, engage in active research, print materials, and host journalists.[73] The research and publications department (CIDOC) was described as "a source of continuing dialogue between the Americas but also an agency for opening this dialogue to Christians everywhere."[74] CIDOC was planned in a way that ensured it would become financially self-sustainable, although in the first years it was funded by CIF New York. The point here is that CIDOC embodied the larger vision Illich had for the church as a prophet and guide in a changing world, namely, making the centres spaces for projected visions of change and actual projects. His framework was the universality of a church incarnated in different cultures.

CIDOC specialized in the collection of books, articles, magazines, and non-published materials with a focus on Latin America and related somehow to the development of religion and ideologies in Latin America; the collection included correspondence with hundreds of people who were preparing manuscripts in those areas. There was a corpus of materials about Latin America going from 1830 to 1959 in relation to the church and its pastoral work in Latin America (about 15,000 items). The centre received 57 periodicals and 230 magazines and had specialized collections on the impact of ideologies and the economy, social change in Latin America, ecclesiology, and school planning.

CIDOC published five series: a) *CIF Reports*, which began in 1961 and by 1965 counted 1,326 subscribers, mostly in Europe and the United States. It published formative materials for prospective missionaries and documents of difficult access related to the church in Latin America and the image created by the church; b) *CIDOC Informa* was at the beginning a twin publication of *CIF Reports* that reproduced the same documents but in their original language (Spanish). In 1965 it changed direction and published *in extenso* the originals of the documents that were used in the preparation of the *CIF Reports*. *CIDOC Informa* had a circulation of 312 copies, mainly in South America; c) *CIF Studies* provided useful statistics on socioreligious changes in Latin America. Three volumes of 300 pages had been published by 1965, and CIDOC expected to sell 800 copies of each; d) *CIDOC Dossier* dealt with the impact of ideologies on the sociocultural options of Latin America,

---

73 "Centre for Intercultural Formation (CIF) Request for Funds" (Cuernavaca, Mexico: CIDOC, c. 1964).
74 The Centre for Intercultural Formation, Cuernavaca, Mexico, Petrópolis, Brazil, Fordham University, NYC, pamphlet, 1965, Daniel Cosío Villegas Library, El Colegio de México, folder 370.196C397d.

and a 300-page volume was expected to be produced at the beginning of 1966; e) *Investigaciones Pastorales* (Pastoral Research) published the results of courses and research done by the Centro de Investigación Pastoral (Centre for Pastoral Research, or CIP).

Illich had a great interest in the pastoral preparation of religious and lay people. On the occasion of a meeting at CIF/CIC during the Pentecost of 1963, which seventeen Latin American bishops attended, CIP was created under the direction of Chilean theologian Segundo Galilea; Bishop Méndez Arceo recognized it as an autonomous centre within CIF and told one of his priests to assist Galilea. Their work during the first two years was used to help the Instituto Pastoral Latinoamericano (ISPLA, known as IPLA), created by CELAM.[75] ISPLA had the goal of educating members of the clergy in the ministry, and the institute was itinerant for a time. The report on the activities of ISPLA in the first two years reads: "More than pastoral courses and ideas already made for the apostles who are already in action, we try to help the clergy to discover for themselves the pastoral ideas and orientations that, in their place and circumstances, God is asking of them. The goal is to help the clergy to form a true 'public opinion', personal, vis a vis the pastoral conjuncture of the church in our continent. In this way, the apostles will be capable to assimilate and incarnate the pastoral orientations and planes, as well as necessary changes in their methodology."[76] CELAM tried to move to the pastors and members of the church theological developments coming from the Vatican Council. Illich wrote a letter to Monsignor Leonidas Proaño, bishop of Riobamba, Ecuador, and president of ISPLA (Centro de Promoción Pastoral del CELAM), asking for advice but suggesting that at that point (August 1965) ISPLA had developed its methodology and was reaching stability and did not need the help of CIP.

For some time the Centre of Information and Development in Latin America (CIDAL), created around 1965 and coordinated from the CIF/CIC Office in Cuernavaca, had a triple function: a) providing assistance to Latin American agencies planning their needs for foreign assistance, b) communication of those needs, and c) lending assistance to "outside" institutions (US, Canadian, and European) in planning their

---

75 "Historia del CIF, 1960–1965" (Cuernavaca, Mexico: CENFI, 1965), Daniel Cosío Villegas Library, El Colegio de México, folder 370.196C397d, 41.

76 Instituto Pastoral Latinoamericano (ISPLA) (Centro de Promoción Pastoral del CELAM), in "Historia del CIF, 1960–1965," Daniel Cosío Villegas Library, El Colegio de México, folder 370.196C397d, 43. See also Ivan Illich to Msgr. Leónidas Proaño, letter, 19 August 1965, in "Historia del CIF, 1960–1965," Daniel Cosío Villegas Library, El Colegio de México, folder 370.196C397d, 51.

collaboration with Latin America and CIDAL. It had a chain of collaborators throughout Latin America.

There was also the CIF Library – this seemed to be referring to CIDOC and to a special collection named the Cardinal Spellman Depository of Documents on the Church and Social Change in Latin America.

The *CIF Reports* – with ten issues a year – were initially conceived as formative tools for future foreign missionaries, introducing Illich's notions of the missioner as rooted in the gospel and a preoccupation with authenticity, self-awareness, and motivation underpinned by the influence of psychoanalysis.[77] They provided information on Latin America. The *Reports*, used both in Cuernavaca and Petrópolis and reaching beyond, became self-financed. They were later compiled in six volumes published by CIDOC in 1969 and 1970 under the series *CIDOC Cuadernos*. From the start, the *Reports* were seen as oriented politically towards a critique of the north, although by and large the texts cannot be considered revolutionary. There is a defensive statement in the January 1963 issue: "CIF Reports is a service with a political platform. Our politics – let us be frank – is to get you involved [in] Latin America. We do not wish to shout with certain extremist groups in either North or Latin America. We only say that we are here, ready to report to you the thinking and activities that have been and are being generated by certain Christian revolutionaries in the Americas."[78]

The tone of the articles and the life of CIF/CIC changed in 1964. In February 1964 Illich took on the role of editor of the *CIF Reports* and announced a change; the board, which included John Considine, was disbanded and an editorial committee created, with Ivan Illich together with his trusted employees and friends Valentina Borremans, director of CIDOC, and Benjamín Ortega.[79] The articles in the *Reports* show a change of direction and of course of content and tone, as we will see.

---

77   "The Centre of Intercultural Formation," Cuernavaca, Mexico, Documento no publicado, Daniel Cosío Villegas Library, El Colegio de México, Inventario 2007, folder 370.196C397d, 18–19. Betsie Hollants directed the *Reports*, Peter Brison was editor, and Renato Poblete was associate researcher.

78   P.V. Brison, "Notes from the Editor: CIF Report I (January 1963)," reprinted in *CIF Reports*, I, April 1962–March 1963, *CIDOC Cuadernos*, xxxvi (Cuernavaca, Mexico: CIDOC, 1969), 8/5.

79   Neither one of them was an active member of the church. Ortega worked on editions of collections published by CIDOC between 1963 and 1976. Valentina Borremans had applied for the position at CIDOC by responding to an advertisement in New York. She took the position of director without any previous experience in a documentation centre.

CENFI

The CIF/CIC in Cuernavaca became very central due to Illich's permanent presence there and the particular micro-cosmos created around it. CIF/CENFI had particular relevance and there were close connections with CIC. The Centro de Formación Intercultural (Centre for Intercultural Formation, or CIF) continued its work after Illich closed CIF/CIC in 1966. CENFI was established as a civil association in Anápolis, Brazil, late in 1960; started to receive participants in 1961; and moved to Petrópolis in the state of Rio in 1962. The courses of eighteen weeks started in January and August and were addressed to priests, religious (women and men), and lay people with a knowledge of English and French and the financial support of their organization. Over the years, it had participants from the United States, Canada, France, Belgium, Germany, Holland, Italy, Ireland, Austria, and Spain. CENFI had a strong message denouncing social injustice, including in its advertising publications statements like: "40% of the total outcome of humanity is in the hands of only 2% of the world population"; "2/3 of mankind [sic] more than two billion human beings – living in constant hunger"; "60% of the population of Latin America is illiterate," and this publication asked next, "Is this Christian?" There was also the following powerful statement: "as Christians: if we fail to fully assume all men [sic], our Christianity is a lie."[80]

There is a paragraph in one CENFI pamphlet that summarizes the overall goal that the centres had developed along the way, notably in paths divergent from the North American hierarchy and the initial promoters. It says: "Christianity, indicating a different path [different from capitalism and communism] for resolving tensions: a profound, intimate change of mentalities and structures in accord with the principles of the social encyclicals, for the first time in history, Christians attempt in Brazil and in the rest of Latin America, to create the society of the future on bases entirely new, bases which correspond to a new and explosive reality."[81]

A major figure in Petrópolis was Bishop Dom Hélder Câmara, auxiliary bishop of Rio and, from 1964, archbishop of Recife and Olinda, referred to in his time as the most impressive figure in the Brazilian church. He was deeply involved in social action, the struggle for human rights after

---

80   CENFI, "The Dimensions of a New World Being Born," no date available,
       information for applicants, Daniel Cosío Villegas Library, El Colegio de México,
       folder 370.1966C397, Tríptico informative.
81   CENFI, "The Dimensions."

the 1964 coup d'état, and of course liberation theology. Illich, in spite of his increasing questioning of the church as institution, the institution-alization of values, and the church's political engagement with the US projects for Latin America, was not engaged in social action. He would not be involved in liberation theology either. He did not embrace a polit-ical ethic of social change. Dom Hélder Câmara, in contrast, was not only a champion of social reform at the Second Session of the Vatican Council. He wanted bishops all over the world to suppress such titles as excellency and eminence and to drop the use of coats of arms and mot-toes, and he rejected the wearing of expensive pectoral crosses and the ring, as well as the use of limousines since these all separated the clergy from the workers and the poor. And of course he rejected the notion of a bishop-prince living in a palace and himself lived humbly. He was involved in actual work in the slums, and he began the first slum eradi-cation in Rio in 1952. Once the people were installed in the new housing project, he organized free classes in all kinds of skills. He then founded the Bank of Providence in Rio, counting on the cooperation of the rich and store owners to keep a clothing bank and make available used fur-niture and medicines; it also offered the services of physicians, lawyers, day labourers, and other professions for free. His social reforms made him controversial.[82] CENFI had this type of sense of social change.

Illich created spaces for emerging ideas in Latin America in his cen-tres. Thus, the encounter of theologians from 2 to 7 March 1964, held in Petrópolis at the CENFI facility, had as its goal the discussion of mutual problems. Participants were Fathers José Comblin, Segundo Galilea, Lucio Gera, Gustavo Gutiérrez, Bonaventure Kloppenburg, Foo Lep-argneur, and Ivan Illich. There were many encounters, but in this one the group was searching for the meaning of Christianity in the context of poverty and oppression in Latin America. Gutiérrez presented a paper in which theology was introduced as "critical reflection on praxis." The original thinking behind liberation theology was discussed.[83]

A MIXED PEDAGOGY: CONSTANCY, HABITS, EXPOSURE, LECTURES,
AND REFLECTION, STILL INSTITUTIONALIZED

Those attending CIF (be it CIC or CENFI) were expected to have an adequate professional formation in the area in which they sought to

---

82 David St-Clair, "The Battling Bishop of Brazil: Dom Hélder Câmara – The Man They Called 'The Electric Mosquito,'" *Les Cloches de Saint-Boniface* 64, no. 2 (February 1965): 86–92, taken from *The Catholic Herald*.

83 Christian Smith, *The Emergence of Liberation Theology: Radical Religion and Social Movement Theory* (Chicago: University of Chicago Press, 1991), 20.

contribute. The purpose of the centre was neither basic professional training nor providing the foundations of their spiritual life; all these were considered prerequisites. The participants were all sponsored by an organization, whether religious or secular, that would guarantee its responsibility for the participant's expenses while at the centre. The centre would provide the skills necessary for participants to communicate the fruit of the profession and their love of God.[84]

Illich strongly believed in the relevance of language, regarding it as a mode of behaviour and as an expression of the culture of the people in whose life the student/missionary wished to participate. CIF proposed that the centre should help the student understand not only the life and culture of Ibero-America, but also his/her/their own life and culture at home, inasmuch as the latter might be an obstacle to effective communication with Latin Americans. Simple translation was not enough.[85] The full value of words, the advertising pamphlet said, cannot be grasped without an understanding of the cultural reality within which the words find their meaning.[86] Therefore, although language training was intense, occupying five hours a day – by other accounts, it was seven hours – with one instructor for three to four students, there was an emphasis placed on understanding the nature of culture. The learning process involved a journey of self-reflection, and the classes went from 8:00 a.m. (at first from 7:30 a.m.) to 9:00 p.m. or 10:00 p.m. The Spanish program used a text and method adapted from that offered by the US State Department for training the State Department Diplomatic Corps and specialized personnel for overseas duty. The course consisted of 450 hours of classroom and laboratory work, in addition to outside study. There were about ten hours a week of lectures, seminars, or other formal class work. Three weekends a month, the participants were assigned to field work. Usually there were one and a half days a month, plus one weekend a month, left free for student leisure.[87] The organigram was similar in Petrópolis, with some variations. The materials and Illich himself do not make mention of Indigenous languages.

84 The Center of Intercultural Formation, Cuernavaca, Mexico; Petrópolis, Brazil; Fordham University, NYC, pamphlet, no date, probably c. 1965, Daniel Cosío Villegas Library, El Colegio de México, folder 370.196C397d, 6.

85 The Center of Intercultural Formation, c. 1965, typed pamphlet, Daniel Cosío Villegas Library, El Colegio de México, folder 370.196C397d.

86 The Center of Intercultural Formation, 12.

87 The Center of Intercultural Formation, Cuernavaca, Mexico; Petropolis, Brazil; Fordham University, NYC 1962–3, pamphlet for publicity, 370.196C397d, 11.

An experiential narration of Benedictine Ambrose Zenner, O.S.B., from Mount Angel Abbey, Oregon, is illustrative of the relevance of CIC (although it is called CIF without differentiating) and of the presence of Méndez Arceo in the life of the centre in Cuernavaca. Zenner, a well-known scholar and doctor in theology from the University of Fribourg, had been sent to Mexico to lead a community foundation in the diocese of Méndez Arceo.[88] Zenner took the course in August 1965 and relates that Méndez Arceo celebrated mass at the Centre of Intercultural Formation. His narration of a very satisfactory experience also reveals an institutionalized learning environment that was more and more enriched with lectures and seminars and firsthand cultural experience. He wrote that during the first week, they were engaged in orientation to every aspect of life in the house and city and that there were leisure hours to become familiar with a community of some 150 people (the number is lower in earlier pamphlets), 60 of whom were priests, and the rest Sisters, with 4 lay papal volunteers. Zenner said: "We priests have to accustom ourselves to wearing ties, and the Sisters to wearing secular dress; to assisting Mass and receiving Communion at times, for the number of those who may concelebrate is limited among so many; to living four in a room with hot water only from 6:00 to 8:00 am, and the demands on the plumbing facilities heavy."[89] (Note that the information for applicants indicates that "in Mexico Sisters may wear their customary habit in the Center, but in order to comply with the desires of the Mexican hierarchy, simple street clothes should be worn on all other occasions.")[90]

The faculty shared by Cuernavaca and Petrópolis, who delivered lectures and spent a few days in the centres, included, from the start, researchers and administrators with different backgrounds, some of

---

88   The narration reads: "Mount Angel Abbey is a Benedictine community founded in 1882 from the Abbey of Engelberg in Switzerland. Situated on a hilltop overlooking Oregon's Willamette Valley, the monks of Mount Angel weave together a place of prayer, hospitality, education, and reflection deeply rooted in the Rule of St. Benedict. Responding to God's call to holiness and preferring nothing whatever to Christ, we dedicate ourselves to a life of prayer and work. We strive to support one another in community, to serve God, the Church, and the larger society. We do this as we celebrate the Holy Eucharist together, pray the Liturgy of the Hours five times daily in choir, and devote ourselves to work, reading, and silence"; see The Monks of Mount Angel Abbey website at https://www.mountangelabbey.org/monastery/. See also Joel Rippinger, *Struggle and Ascent: The History of Mount Angel Abbey* (Minnesota: Liturgical Press, 2020).

89   Ambrose Zenner, O.S.B., "The First Two Months," dated November 1965, folder 370.196C397d.

90   Zenner, "The First Two Months."

whom had been close to Illich, some with strong institutional roles. This was the case with Everett Reimer, who at the time (as per the 1962 calendar) was a member of the Junta de Planificación (Economic Planning Board) in San Juan, Puerto Rico; Dr. Remy Bastien, the director of the Inter-American School of Applied Social Sciences of the Organization of American States; Jesuit Father Emile Pin, a professor of religious sociology at Pontifical Gregorian University, Rome; and Jesuit Father Joseph P. Fitzpatrick, chairman of the Department of Social Sciences at Fordham University, New York, among others. There were not radical figures on the list in contrast with those lecturing from 1965 and onwards, as we will see.

The curricular materials published in the first two years of the *CIF Reports*, from April 1962 to March 1964, pose to the participants the question of the time: whether the work of the church should be palliative and relieve spiritual and material hardship – through charity and welfare work – or whether the church should encourage reform and actual change of existing social conditions. These approaches represented the political positioning of different sectors of the church and were delineated in their understanding of and relationship between charity and justice. This had been already under discussion in the late 1920s and 1930s. Once again concerned with infusing Catholic values, the materials explored the pastoral methods required to take care of urban masses and give them an identity as a Christian (Catholic) community.[91] Other questions also emerged: Is a Christian community possible in the slums? Will religious missionaries live there?[92] The questioning was accompanied by hard data on land distribution, life in the slums, education, and level of illiteracy. The *Reports* were written in Cuernavaca and had associate editors as well as advisors from Canada, the United States, and Latin America.

The articles, originating in various Latin American countries and other parts of the world as well, reflected the social positioning of local (Catholic) churches and their relation to social movements, conveyed the epistemic turn in theology, and captured political utopias and projects in

---

91 Some paragraphs included in this chapter come from Rosa Bruno-Jofré and Jon Igelmo Zaldívar, "The Center for Intercultural Formation, Cuernavaca, Mexico: Its Reports (1962–1967) and Illich's Critical Understanding of Mission in Latin America," *Hispania Sacra* LXV, Extra II (July–December 2013), 7–31, doi:10.3989kkkk/hs2014.034.

92 CIC, 1962, "Facts That Pose Questions about Latin America," in *CIF Reports*, vol. 1, April 1962–March 1963: 1/13, *CIDOC Cuaderno*, no. 36 (Cuernavaca, Mexico: CIDOC, 1969).

gestation. They also brought in voices from people in the field. Thus, a 1963 article contains a quotation from members of a Peace Corps team, trained at University of Notre Dame and at the *Instituto de Educacíon Rural* (Rural Education Institute) in Chile, echoing a statement of principle that is in line with the *Reports* and reproduced there: "We are not leaders in these projects; we are there to help the leaders in any way they decide we can help."[93] In the same article, the author includes a pastoral letter from Chilean Bishop Bernardino Piñera, written in 1962, that embodies a current in the Latin American church, the roots of which in Chile went back to the 1930s and earlier: "Finally, our analysis suggests that we must always disentangle ourselves a little more from established institutions, avoid costly buildings, complex organizations, works that require and involve a lot of money, and recuperate the spiritual vitality of primitive times ... Our times are more those of catechism and missions than of schools and colleges, times of humble chapels in the slums not of sumptuous temples, times of hermitages not rich monasteries. And, although it seems paradoxical, it is preferable that we be seen as poor rather than as benefactors of the poor."[94]

This is a critique of the class bias of Catholic institutions, in particular schools, and of the costly bureaucracies as well as the missionaries acting as mediators. The critique is not far from Illich's argument – showing that we need to be careful not to decontextualize Illich's positioning as unique to him. The statement by the bishop was grounded in the notion of a simple spirituality rooted in the community, as in early Christianity, and embedded in social reality and in the life world. It was a matter of incarnating "poverty" rather than charity; there was a quest for authenticity at this point when existentialism as well as personalism were influential among Catholics in Latin America, and for a language of justice. Structural issues were on the table for discussion. In fact, the themes for missionaries in Cuernavaca and Petrópolis, contained in the *CIF Reports* during the period of 1962–4, included socio-economic problems in Latin America, such as unjust land distribution, internal migration to cities, slums, and illiteracy. The materials are organized through questions that ask the future missionary, for example, what does it all mean for the church? What are the answers to the problems in light of the role of demagogues? Who uses the means of communication? How do we deal with ignorance?

---

93 Fr. W. McKeon, "The Church in Chile: A Visit to a Country in Crisis," 1963, *CIF Reports*, vol. 1, April 1962–March 1963: 3/24, *CIDOC Cuaderno*, no. 36 (Cuernavaca, Mexico: CIDOC, 1969).
94 McKeon, "The Church in Chile," 3–28.

The readings also critique the church in Latin America as following a European model, with its monumental structures, schools, welfare, press, and formation movements, and for how it did not always count on financial support from governments but relied on donations from the wealthy. Within this context, the poor, it is concluded, did not have a sense of belonging to the church or a sense of building up the church.

The centres intended, as a fundamental initial goal, to generate a missionary education program, and many of the missionaries were to be involved in community programs, literacy work, and community education. However, there was no specific construction of the understanding of community education, but instead narrations of practices. An article by Mariana Bandeira, published in the *Report* in 1962, reads:

> Basic education, according to the Movement for Grassroots Education (MEB) is designed to help the student open his [*sic*] eyes and to discover and understand his [*sic*] own problems and to do so effectively and on his [*sic*] own initiative. It is a special type of education of adults; it is not directed solely to the need of the students to read, write and know technical matters necessary for their work. The MEB also has the mission of helping men [*sic*] to understand their social situation that conditions their life and their destiny. In order that we may understand the matter better let us use the word "conscientization", that is, man's [*sic*] training and "effectivization" to the point where [s/he] is able to take account of himself [*sic*] as a human being, of his [*sic*] problems, and of his [*sic*] duties and rights, including the right to fight for a fair and just solution to his [*sic*] problems.[95]

Of course this is in line with Paulo Freire's vision of literacy and adult education, which is not surprising since Freire was involved in the movement and was at the time the director of the University of Recife's Cultural Extension Service. Illich met Freire through Hélder Câmara early in the 1960s, probably 1962. Freire led the implementation of what was known later as Método Paulo Freire (Method) in literacy programs for thousands of peasants in the northeast of Brazil, a practice nourished by the environment and the concepts developed in Brazil at the time. The very notion of conscientization, central to Freire's early pedagogical theory, is attributed to Câmara.[96]

---

95 Bandeira, "MEB – 'Movimento de Educação de Base,'" 1/12.
96 Illich related that he intervened through Teodoro Moscoso, who had been one of the five members of the board of higher education in Puerto Rico, where they served together, along with the administrator of the Alliance for Progress, to liberate Freire

The missionary engaged in the pastoral renewal advocated by Illich was expected to understand the milieu where she would develop her apostolate and recognize the virtues not incorporated in pastoral formulations: "solidarity, hospitality, generosity, and adaptability of this same miserable proletariat."[97] In other words, the missioner needed to be attentive to the local church and to the way people lived Christianity and the virtues they cultivated. The text went on to say that "where pastoral renewal has taken the care to put these values in perspective and unite them to the sacramental life of the parish community very encouraging results have been obtained."[98] There is an insistence on the need for a new pastoral theology, one that pursues an "authentic Christianity" – a Christianity rooted in the human structure of society, in societies where there is even a religious mix-up, that is, a form of syncretism.[99] This approach would take shape in Vatican II documents with an emphasis on the local church, still with a universal conversionist tone of truth.

We read in a 1962 *Report* that the task and the church's role is "to order that man's [*sic*] dignity be respected and that society be organized in a way in which the minimum of comfort – without which the practice of virtue is impossible or difficult – be promoted."[100] Another article of the same year moves the argument to the issue of rapid de-Christianization; the missioner needs to counter the forces promoting this process, which are also the forces offering a solution to injustices. It is a matter of Catholics responding effectively, the text says, to the spiritual, religious, cultural, and social demands of the situation. Economic underdevelopment cannot be overcome only in economic terms; it is fundamental to move the spiritual forces: "The essence of the Christian message contains the whole answer."[101]

The missionaries were then entrusted with a political-spiritual role, to help "apply in their entirety the social teachings of the church, as

---

from jail after the military coup that overthrew João Gourlart. Moscoso intervened on behalf of Paulo Freire and peasant leader Francisco Julião. Illich had met Freire a year and a half before. See Cayley, *Ivan Illich in Conversation*, 205–6.

97   CIC, 1962, "The Church and Catholics in Latin America," in *CIF Reports*, vol. 1, April 1962–March 1963: 1/22, *CIDOC Cuaderno*, no. 36 (Cuernavaca, Mexico: CIDOC, 1969).

98   CIC, 1962, "The Church and Catholics."

99   CIF, 1963, "The Future of 'Cristianismo' in Latin America," in *CIF Reports*, vol. 2, April 1963–March 1964: 2/24, *CIDOC Cuaderno*, no. 37 (Cuernavaca, Mexico: CIDOC, 1969).

100   CIC, 1962, "Facts That Pose Questions about Latin America," 1/22.

101   CIC, 1962, "The Church and Catholics," 1/23.

explained at the Center, and to diffuse among the faithful charity and the love of justice," as the solution for Latin America. However, although there is no mention of specific papal documents or political parties, the call includes a normative statement: "the continent's social structures were no longer suited to the conditions of development."[102] They needed to be transformed, for example, to institute land reform, initiate social legislation, and respond to all new aspirations of the people. It is not surprising, then, that the situation in Chile had a special place in the materials for missionary formation (printed in the first two years of the *Reports*), and later on in the collection of articles published as *Reports*.

The Chilean Christian Democratic Party had been founded in 1957 and in 1958, with its candidate Eduardo Frei, an admirer of Jacques Maritain, reaching national prominence when he received a substantial number of votes. The party moved to create a powerful Catholic grassroots network made up of neighbourhood committees, mothers' groups, and youth clubs in many slums. It was an example of community development, and the party leaders claimed that both capitalism and socialism could be transcended in a communitarian society, a concept that was not clearly defined. It was an attempt at social reform, including agrarian reform, combined with a strong attachment to democracy, and was encapsulated in the phrase "a revolution in liberty."[103] There was a great deal of hope around the ideas expounded by the Christian Democratic Party, although Illich was cautious since he did not support the idea of developing European-style Christian Democratic parties in Latin America. He tried to rescue the uniqueness of each place and its people, as the Catholicity of the church resides in assuming and embodying differences.

The formative texts in the *Reports* do not spare the church. It needed its own reform and also needed to reorient its pastoral work according to the demands of the time: "She must be present among men [*sic*] of all times to lead them to God's eternal kingdom."[104]

Overall, the *Reports* published between 1962 and 1964 contain articles in line with the rhetoric of the Cold War and include the concern with Cuba, an analysis of Catholic education in Latin America, and studies regarding the need to extend Catholic education at a time of demographic changes in the congregations, as shown by the decline in

---

102   CIC, 1962, "The Church and Catholics," 1/23.

103   Simon Collier and William F. Sater, *A History of Chile, 1808–2002*, 2nd ed. (Cambridge: Cambridge University Press, 2004), 307.

104   CIC, 1962, "The Church and Catholics," 1/23.

vocations. The articles also address difficulties in the process of adaptation of the church's structures to contemporary societal demands, with specific references to schooling, technology, and the use of reason and freedom. The *Reports* call for a "proper proportion" between theology of redemption and theology of incarnation, which is "clarified" in a gendered language as "a matter of appreciating the passive and active, the 'feminine' and 'masculine' character of man [*sic*] and his [*sic*] society."[105] This statement is in line with the inherited Greek (Aristotelian) tradition of positioning the woman as only man's passive "underling" – a theory adopted by Thomas Aquinas and the scholastic tradition.[106]

The Alliance for Progress was a central macro-component of the context presented to missionaries, who were introduced to the various readings of its concept and implementation in 1962–4. Thus, through the use of quotations, the editor organized an imaginary roundtable around the questions: "What would your over-all estimate be of the Alliance for Progress now completing its second year?"[107] It included a range of opinions that were expressions of political positionings with reference to Latin America: Hélder Câmara, who was quoted as saying, "Liberty is only a name, a sound for the two thirds of mankind, without houses, without clothes, without food, without a minimum of education and above all without human conditions";[108] Father Vekemans, a Belgian Jesuit working in Chile and supporter of the Christian Democratic Party; Teodoro Moscoso, US coordinator for the Alliance for Progress; and João Goulart, the president of Brazil deposed by a coup in 1964, among others.[109] The point here was for the missionary to become familiar with the political forces working in Latin America, the conceptual spaces containing social and political positions, and contesting visions around change, including the notion of revolution (from the

---

105   Peter Brison, "Notes from the Editors of CIF Reports," November 1962; reprinted in *CIF Reports*, vol. 1, April 1962–March 1963, *CIDOC Cuaderno*, no. 36 (Cuernavaca, Mexico: CIDOC, 1969), 6/4. These issues are also discussed in Rosa Bruno-Jofré and Jon Igelmo Zaldívar, "Ivan Illich, the Critique of the Church as It: From a Vision of the Missionary to a Critique of Schooling, in *Catholic Education in the Wake of Vatican II*, ed. Rosa Bruno-Jofré and Jon Igelmo Zaldívar (Toronto: University of Toronto Press, 2017), 135–52.

106   Lea Boutin, MO, *Women in the Church: The Pain, the Challenge, the Hope* (Aurora, ON: Southdown Emmanuel Convalescent Foundation, 1991), 9.

107   CIC, 1963, "The 'Alliance in Progress,'" *CIF Reports*, vol. 2, April 1963–March 1964: 3/6, *CIDOC Cuaderno*, no. 37 (Cuernavaca, Mexico: CIDOC, 1969).

108   CIC, 1963, "The 'Alliance in Progress,'" 3/9.

109   CIC, 1963, "The 'Alliance in Progress,'" 3/10.

Marxist perspective, to the reformist one of revolution in freedom, to Kennedy's notion of "revolution").

Breaking Bonds

From 1964, after Illich took control of the *Reports*, they also reproduced articles that brought in a language of denunciation and demands for social justice and radical changes. Such was the case of an article by Francisco Julião, a Brazilian lawyer and peasant leader from northeast Brazil, as well as the founder of the Ligas Camponesas, co-founder of the Brazilian Socialist Party, and a friend of Illich. Julião denounced the industry of anti-communism, its surrounding publicity, and its discourse that portrayed the left as harassing the Christian family and introducing foreign systems. He wrote: "For these last-minute 'saviours', the 'Christian family' is the one of the landowner who, in every country, arms himself with a rifle and a machine gun in order to defend, like a feudal lord, his property rights in the land ... Brazil, 'Christian country', is underdeveloped, underfed, and oppressed ... I do not believe that my country will be freed by the elections. Nor by the elite. Nor by the Christian family. I will be liberated, and of this I am sure, by the desperate masses, by the worker without land."[110]

After 1964 the articles in the *Reports* contained alternative radicalized grassroots experiences and political reflections, which were at odds with the conception of social change sustained by the hierarchy of the US church, in particular by Archbishop Cushing, the NCWC's Latin American Bureau, and US policymakers. This was a discourse and practice grounded in the modernization of Latin America and in line with US policies within the framework of the Cold War, which included some reforms such as agrarian reform and the militarization of the regions following the US national security agenda.

From soon after Illich took control of the editorial board, we find an article titled "Subversion through Catholic Education?" (1964), written by Marina Bandeira, executive director of the radio school system of the Bishops of Brazil and secretary of MEB. The article introduces MEB and the events surrounding the confiscation of the primer *Viver é Lutar* in 1964 by the conservative governor of the state of Guanabara, Carlos Lacerda. Bandeira's article represented education not as a service offered by the church, but as a tool for subversion. Notably, it was published before

---

110 Francisco Julião, "Brazil. 'Christian Country,'" in *CIF Reports*, vol. 3, April–December 1964: 1/11, *CIDOC Cuaderno*, no. 38 (Cuernavaca, Mexico: CIDOC, 1970). Originally published in *Monthly Review Press* (September 1962): 243–50.

the end of Vatican II.[111] Illich's language and concerns moved towards a critique of the church as institution, the church as It, although not towards a critique of the patriarchal character of the church as It. Illich's critique of the church as institution would reach a high point in 1967.

The centres and Illich reflected the political and cultural revolts of the 1960s in the United States and Europe and the overall social movements of the global 1960s. But, very specially, the articles were nourished by changes coming from the South itself and the interaction with Cuernavaca, a hub of ideas and a rich micro-cosmos. The visions of change from the South were part of the lived experience, the reception of Vatican II, the critique of American policies that emerged from missionary work in the field – such as the case of the Maryknolls from the late 1960s – and the intensity of social and political movements in Latin America. There was a movement from South to North in terms of alternative visions of the role of the church in Latin America.

There was a change in political direction embodied in the origin and content of the articles reprinted in the *CIF Reports*. Between 1964 and 1967, the *Reports* show an interest in the grassroots experiences in Latin America as well as the political movement, including the growing influence of the Christian Democratic Party in Chile. We also find articles by Marina Bandeira, mentioned before; Hélder Câmara, archbishop of Olinda and Recife and outspoken representative of liberation theology; Francisco Julião, peasant leader and representative from MEB; Carlos Fuentes, Mexican writer; Ivan Vallier, sociologist at Berkeley; José María Sbert, Mexican writer; Salvador Allende, who would become the first Socialist president of Chile; and Eduardo Frei, who went on to be the Christian Democratic president of Chile. The *Reports* also printed Adolfo Gilly's "Camilo Torres: His Program," first published in *MARCHA* (Montevideo); Eduardo Galeano's "Che Guevara: His Commitment," reproduced from the *Monthly Review*, a journal of the new left; Vicente Lombardo Toledano's "Marxism and the Sacred Texts: Three Sermons," taken from *Siempre* (Mexico); and Gregorio Lemercier's "A Benedictine Monastery and Psychoanalysis," reproduced from *Le Monde*.[112]

---

111   Marina Bandeira, "Movimento de Educaçao de Base," a report given to the Catholic Inter-American Cooperation Program (CICOP), Chicago, 23 February 1964. *CIF Reports*, vol. 3, April–December 1964. Reprinted in *CIDOC Cuadernos*, no. 38 (Cuernavaca, Mexico: CIDOC, 1970). See also Andrew Dawson, "A Very Brazilian Experiment: The Base Education Movement 1961–1967," *History of Education* 31, no. 2 (November 2010): 185–94; Scott Mainwaring, *The Catholic Church and Politics in Brazil, 1916–1985* (Stanford, CA: Stanford University Press, 1986).
112   Bruno-Jofré and Igelmo Zaldívar, "Monsignor Ivan Illich's Critique."

We also noticed an expansion of the list, in 1964 and 1965, of those delivering lectures and seminars. Some of the names were Father Gustavo Gutiérrez, leading Peruvian theologian of liberation theology; Jesuit Father Juan Luis Segundo, Uruguayan theologian of liberation theology; Father Camilo Torres Restrepo, revolutionary priest from Colombia who died in action; Bishop Sergio Méndez Arceo; Everett Reimer; Chilean Jesuit Alejandro del Corro, who worked with the disposed in Santiago and with the Hogar de Cristo; Brazilian Archbishop Hélder Pessoa Câmara; Argentinian Jesuit Father Alberto Sily, social activist involved in union struggles; and American Michael Maccoby, anthropologist, psychoanalyst, and expert in leadership. These lecturers who spent some time with those taking the course were the avantgarde of change and embodied radical, transformative Catholic social visions. Some of the titles are quite suggestive: "Social Change and Its Impact on Education in Latin America"; "Studying the Contribution of Private Medical Services in Latin America: Medical Services and Apostolate"; "Continuation of EduPlan I, Christology in Latin America," etc.[113]

Contextualizing Illich's Shift

The "long 1960s"[114] was characterized by a political and cultural constellation with many fronts, political conjunctures, religious intersections, and a new sense of being. Vatican II (1962–5) and its renewal process had an impact from the time of its preparation on the life of the religious communities and the church, while liberation theology developed in Latin America with reflections grounded in the reality of oppressed people.[115] The divide was no longer along the lines of liberals and conservatives; there was a relationship between radical politics and theology – a theology of liberation. The Catholic hierarchy in North America was quite aloof to the changes, but the centres in Cuernavaca were in the thick of things.

The New Left had a voice, and the Cuban Revolution was a point of reference in Latin America, where the United States intervened to assert its control, often through coups d'état. The Cold War provided the context. The civil rights movement and its legacy went well beyond

---

113 "Historia del CIF," folder 370.196C397d, 30–7.
114 Arthur Marwick, *The Sixties: Cultural Revolution in Britain, France, Italy, and the United States, c.1958–c.1974* (Oxford: Oxford University Press, 1988).
115 Christian Smith, *The Emergence of Liberation Theology: Radical Religion and Social Movement Theory* (Chicago: University of Chicago Press, 1991).

the boundaries of the north, while second-wave feminism opened a new understanding of gender relations to which the church remained hostile. Illich himself received strong criticism later, when he published his book *Gender* in the early 1980s. Feminist thea/o/*logy appeared a bit later.

It was also a time of secularization – this did not imply erasing religion since new forms of Christianity took shape – and pluralism, which indeed became a challenge to religious faith, because contamination relativizes.[116] There was indeed a revolt against Christian cultural oppression, including women's oppression; an extensive rejection of external authority that included the church; and ongoing changes in societal values, including the rise of individualism, which was not alien to changes in the capitalist system. Further differentiation in the functioning of institutions, including the engagement of the church in social services, influenced the consciousness of individuals.[117] Of course, as it normally happened in this kind of context, there was a perceived crisis of the education system, with the points made ranging from issues of inequality to radical critiques of schooling (Paul Goodman, John Holt) to poor formation in science after the launch of *Sputnik* by the Soviet Union to new ways of practising education, as was the case with literacy and adult education in the South. A number of teaching congregations, particularly women congregations, had left the classroom by the end of the decade.

Vatican II started to generate substantial changes in the Catholic programs and in the life of the congregations. It was a change of paradigm. Illich, in spite of participating in the second and third sessions of the council and serving as an advisor to the committee of four cardinals, appointed by Paul VI to moderate the council, was disappointed with Vatican II.[118] Hartch argued that Illich's experience had changed his attitudes towards church authorities. The tuning with modernity was not close to Illich's heart. The theologians of Vatican II left aside Thomism, something dear to Illich, and neo-scholasticism and moved to a theology in tune with the modern world and valuing human experience and relationality.[119] Furthermore, the politics of the church disturbed him.

116   These comments are based on Rosa Bruno-Jofré, "The 'Long 1960s' in a Global Arena of Contention: Re-defining Assumptions of the Self, Morality, Race, Gender, and Justice and Questioning Education," *Espacio, Tiempo y Educación* (Scopus Journal) 6, no. 1 (2019): 5–27, Spain.

117   Bruno-Jofré, "The 'Long 1960s.'"

118   Hartch, *The Prophet of Cuernavaca*, 65; Cayley, *Rivers North of the Future*, 7–8.

119   Michael Attridge, "From Objectivity to Subjectivity: Changes in the Nineteenth and Twentieth Centuries and Their Impact on Post-Vatican II Theological Education,"

The tension with the Holy See was building up, but Illich had Cardinal Spellman's protection. Illich was clear cut on important issues, and he read the times with overlapping lenses, as we will explain. Situating himself outside the agenda of the North American hierarchy, in 1965, Illich wrote an open letter to the national director of PAVLA, Raymond A. Kevane, and all the PAVLA directors. Illich's stated intention was to help PAVLA to rethink its institutional purposes and protect CIF from attacks by those who were critical of the acceptance of PAVLA volunteers. In the letter, he actually explains why the principal purpose of PAVLA – to motivate US Catholics to volunteer services to the church in Latin America, to elicit support for them, and to raise cash – is prejudicial to the church of 1965. For a fraction of the cost of a volunteer, including orienting inefficient and temporary voluntary help, local personnel with greater usable experience and higher qualifications could be employed. Volunteers are tolerated, he wrote, for the wrong reasons. Illich advised that PAVLA be discontinued and made into a foundation.[120]

His critique of PAVLA makes sense within the context of Illich's understanding of a universal church rooted in locality and culture and his notion of the missionary, and in light of the sociopolitical context of Latin America in 1965. CIDOC, created in 1963, as Jon Igelmo argued, had become more and more prominent, and Illich had somewhat left aside the other centres.[121] Illich had taken control of the *CIF Reports* in 1964, as we examined, generating important changes in their content. The conservative Catholic clergy in Mexico was concerned about Illich. An incident with the Oficio Catequístico de la Arquidiócesis de Mexico in the summer of 1966 that revealed the influence of psychoanalysis, and that will be examined in the next chapter, set the stage for further confrontation with the Holy See at a time when Illich and CIDOC were critical of the Catholic Church as an institution. In October 1966 Illich asked Bishop Méndez Arceo of Cuernavaca for permission to merge the centres into one – the Centro Intercultural de Documentación

---

in *Catholic Education in the Wake of Vatican II*, ed. Rosa Bruno-Jofré and Jon Igelmo Zaldívar (Toronto: University of Toronto Press, 2017), 21–43.

120   Letter from Ivan Illich to Rev. Raymond A. Kevane, National Director, Pavla, Cuernavaca, 27 April 1965. At the top of the document it reads: "This letter is being reproduced for study at a 'Methods and Problems of Intercultural Sensibility Development Workshop', December 27 to January 5, 1966."

121   Jon Igelmo Zaldívar, "Ivan Illich en el CIDOC (Centro Intercultural de Documentación de Cuernavaca, 1963–1976. Un Acontecimiento para la Genealogia de la Educación" (PhD diss., Faculty of Education, Universidad Complutense de Madrid, 2011), 122.

Figure 2.3. 1960s decade montage.

Source: Licensed under the Creative Commons Attribution – Share Alike 3.0, a work by CatJar, from a variety of images credited above (Blackcat replaced two images not reliable for Commons), (creativecommons.org/licenses/by-sa/3.0), via Wikimedia Commons, available at https://commons.wikimedia.org/wiki/File:1960s_decade _montage.png.

(CIDOC) – and move to Rancho Tetela, and to cease to offer residence to the missionaries.

In September 1966, he wrote in an internal document that CIF began with the aim of serving as a catalyst within the Roman Catholic Church and saw itself as part of a continued occasion for the development of consciousness around ecclesiastic interdependence between South America, the United States, Canada, and Europe. It had, he wrote, ceased to operate as such. He thought it had been very quickly cast into the role of meeting place and mediator between Latin American groups whose opposed ideologies frequently made it difficult for them to meet on matters of common concern. Illich then quotes something he stated in 1964, the year he took control of the *Reports*: "We are always ahead of our times and always only temporary and ephemeral. We should never think that what we start should continue the way we started it. We should not think that our organization should last a long time." He concludes with: "We hope that the major legacy transmitted by CIF to the groups, publications, programs or institutions it has helped to develop is the joyful detachment from permanence."[122]

---

122 Ivan Illich, "Definition of CIF," typed one-page document, September 1966, Daniel Cosío Villegas Library, El Colegio de México, folder 370.1996C397v.

3 CIDOC as an Independent Intellectual Hub and the Conflict with the Church

Making CIDOC an Independent Intellectual Hub

In 1966 Ivan Illich closed a chapter in his complex political relationship with the Latin American Bureau of the National Catholic Welfare Conference, and with John Considine, Cardinal Cushing, and other members of the US hierarchy, as well as with Fordham University. However, he would maintain close ties with the controversial Cardinal Spellman, who would continue to protect him. To an important extent, the break was a natural process as much as a re-accommodation to a new historical context, and it was a political repositioning of Illich himself. Through CIF, he had started and consolidated CIDOC, making it self-sustainable, and it became an independent hub for activities and key thinkers of the time. In CIDOC's early years in the new setting, Illich would enter into a broad dialogue that came from his theological Catholic perspective, grounded in the gospel and a critique of the church, in making his case for the corruption of Catholic virtues.

CIDOC was registered as a Civil Mexican Association with a board of directors and with Illich as president in the state of Morelos,[1] located

---

1 The members of the board of directors were Ramon Xirau, professor of philosophy and literature, Universidad Autónoma de México; Manuel Alcalá, former director of the National Library, and at the time Mexican ambassador to UNESCO, Paris; Guillermo Margadant, director of the Seminar on Roman Law (Derecho Romano), Universidad Autónoma de México; and Michael Maccoby, researcher in social psychology. Valentina Borremans was executive secretary of the board of directors and signed on as director of CIDOC. See Valentina Borremans, to Rev. Mr. Dr. Dom Cándido Padim and R.P. Lucio Gera and those listening, Mexico, D.F., 25 September 1967, in Tarsicio Ocampo, ed., *Mexico: "Entredicho" del Vaticano a CIDOC 1966–1969*, *CIDOC Dossier*, no. 37 (Cuernavaca, Mexico: CIDOC, 1969), 4/37. Informe for CELAM. In the letter, Borremans was responding to questions posed by the visitors

in Casa Blanca del Rancho Tetela on the hills west of Cuernavaca. The offices of CIP and ISPLA (that, as Illich said, "were dependent from the hierarchy") moved to their own locations; they did not go with CIDOC to Rancho Tetela.[2] Illich wrote: "My insistence [that they be separated] had as objective to underscore the complete lay character of our activities moved to Rancho Tetela, fully freed from any ecclesiastical tie."[3]

CIDOC would not be a residence in situ for prospective missionaries and volunteers as CIF/CIC had been. It did not have a semi-public chapel, as the Hotel Chulavista had provided. This underscored not only the lay character of CIDOC, but, as Illich asserted, its independence from the clergy. He actually disassociated CIDOC from every power and clerical jurisdiction, and during the conflict with the Vatican, he would request to be liberated from ecclesiastical ministry. However, as we will see, he remained faithful to the church as It and to the doctrine and magisterium of the church, as per his statements, and not necessarily only to the church as She, in reference to the tradition, the spirituality, and its apostolate. His differentiation of the church as It and the church as She may help in comprehending his vision of schooling as an institution and his differentiation of schooling from education. However, in his institutional critique, he did not want to destroy the church as institution; he critiqued the institution from the standpoint of his Catholicism and the Catholic virtues (disposing agents to good actions) as a moral theologian, all within the Thomist framework.

CIDOC was, to an important extent, the cradle of Illich's analysis of modern institutions, and in our case of schooling and education, even if we place this analysis in relation to many semantic layers and experiential and intellectual threads. These layers show overlapping meanings and concepts that brought different temporalities to his thinking – from the magisterium, scholastic theology and the distrust of modernity, and phenomenology, through to Thomas Aquinas and some ideas from neomedievalism (that can be associated to his questioning of the role of the state), to psychoanalysis, critical theology, radical critiques of US policies, and the meaning he made of his own experiences at various times. Of relevance here is the relationship with Everett Reimer, whom he met in Puerto Rico, as we mentioned before, and who he was reunited with

---

from CELAM, there to conduct an investigation to be submitted to Exmo. Sr. Avelar Brandao Vilela, president of CELAM.

2 Ivan Illich, letter to Sergio Méndez Arceo, Bishop of Cuernavaca, 24 June 1966, in Tarsicio Ocampo, ed., *Mexico: "Entredicho" del Vaticano a CIDOC 1966–1969, CIDOC Dossier*, no. 37 (Cuernavaca, Mexico: CIDOC, 1969), 4/107.

3 Illich to Méndez Arceo, 24 June 1966, 4/107; free translation.

again in 1967 at CIDOC; they collaborated for some time on a prospective book with the provisional title *Alternatives in Education* that did not come to fruition.

We will now briefly introduce CIDOC to provide the context for the background setting of *Deschooling Society*. As a centre, CIDOC worked on the documentation and analysis of the influence of ideologies on socio-economic change in Latin America and operated as a kind of open university and intellectual and political hub. It published *CIDOC Dossier*, a collection of sources for the study of ideologies and social change in Latin America;[4] *CIDOC Sondeos*, a publication that promoted further research on the religious phenomenon in Latin America (CIDOC published thirty volumes annually), which was distributed mainly to universities and research centres; *CIDOC Archivos*, an annual catalogue of the collection of materials for the study of churches and beliefs in Latin America from 1830, whose subscribers had access to archived materials through its reproduction service; and *CIDOC Informa*, with a limited circulation, which reproduced documents for the study of public opinion about the church and other religious institutions in Latin America.[5] In addition, *CIDOC Cuadernos* reproduced readings used in the seminaries and courses as well as information on encounters and comments made in the discussions. The *Cuadernos* reproduced entire collections, such as the *CIF Reports*.[6] The courses, conferences, seminars, and the school of language were ebullient sites that reached out to Latin America, Europe, and beyond. The Institute for the Study of Transformation of Contemporary Latin America offered many specialized courses that were recognized as credits by major US universities; in 1967–8, it offered thirty-four of those courses. The Cycle of Orientation on Latin America, a series of 180 public presentations/lectures, films, and exhibitions, was addressed to university students (missionaries, technical assistants) willing to work in Latin America. Sixty of those presentations were on the following topics: sociocultural transformation in Latin America; the role of religions in this process; and

---

4 CIDOC published fifteen volumes per year of *CIDOC Dossier*, each one having 200–500 pages and a bibliography of 500–1,500 citations. Each *Dossier* addressed a current particular controversy. See Borremans to Cándido Padim and Lucio Gera and those listening, Mexico, 25 September 1967, 4/37.

5 Borremans to Cándido Padim and Lucio Gera and those listening, Mexico, 25 September 1967, 4/36 and 4/37.

6 Jon Igelmo Zaldívar, "Ivan Illich en el CIDOC (Centro Intercultural de Documentación de Cuernavaca, 1963–1976: Un acontecimiento para la genealogia de la educación" (PhD diss., Faculty of Education, Universidad Complutense de Madrid, 2011), 163.

research tools in both areas. The Escuela de Idiomas (Language School) was of great importance. It focused on the teaching of Spanish, and it had between 50 and 250 students from the United States, Canada, and Europe, with half of them typically attending other courses offered by CIDOC.[7]

The Critique of the Institutional Church: The Church as It

From the start of Illich's work in Cuernavaca, the conservative Mexican bishops and political elements felt uncomfortable with his work, ideas, and relationships, but the intensive summer course on catechesis (from 11 July to 19 August 1966) became a turning point. This would have consequences for Illich's relationship with the Holy See. The summer course was organized by the Oficio Catequístico de la Arquidiócesis de México through the Instituto Catequístico Sedes Sapientiae and was for women and men religious as well as the public. The institute invited Father Segundo Galilea, who was in charge of the Centre for Pastoral Research (CIP), the centre related to CIF/CIC, and Father Jesús Torres, director of the Equipo Pastoral de la Unión de Ayuda Mutua Episcopal (UMAE), to collaborate for parts of the program. Galilea brought himself and members of CIF (as stated in the report), Monsignor Ivan Illich; Monsignor Víctor Nazario; Father Ceslaus (Lee) Hoinacki, O.P.; Father Claude Bayeux; and Deacon Julio Torres. The presentations by members of the team related to CIP and CIF made statements mostly dealing with religious vocations and containing aggressive analogies and metaphors that referred to the search for purity in vocations and the need to remove masks that often took the form of religious practices. The director of the Oficio Catequístico, Monsignor Francisco Aguilera, following instructions from the archbishop of Mexico, submitted his serious objections in a letter to the papal nuncio. The following are some of the phrases included in the letter, some of which fall within a patriarchal construction of womanhood and spirituality.

Ceslaus Hoinacki, O.P., is quoted as saying: "Without loving experiences it is impossible to carry out a mature religious life. These experiences are necessary before entering religious life for a conscious surrendering. Those [women religious] who entered without having those experiences should leave and come back with a better knowledge of what they do ... That all [referring to the Sisters] should marry.

---

7 Borremans to Cándido Padim and Lucio Gera and those listening, Mexico, 25 September 1967, 4/36.

The vows of religious life destroy the personality and form abnormal human beings ... Community life in seminaries and religious congregations destroy the personality."[8]

Monsignor Victor Nazario is quoted as saying:

Women religious today are not useful to the world. There is lots of religious ignorance due to the egoism of women religious secluded in convents ... Mass is a commerce; it is scandalous to celebrate three masses ... Female [femenina] religious life could develop, in groups of married people, who meet periodically to have a more intense spiritual life, and a common apostolate. The vow of chastity is not necessary ... The royalty of Christ is an error ... One can only talk of royalty in a monarchic context, but the church embodies democratic people of equals ... this is why we can only talk of Christ as a good Pastor.[9]

Father Claude Bayeux is quoted as saying: "We have made the Church an ensemble of superstitions and anarchy because we charge to baptize small children, we force the faithful to take communion too much, to engage devotions to saints, [and to] give alms only for the economic protection of the priest and the religious."[10]

Monsignor Illich referred to women religious: "The woman religious should have a heart capable of universal love and for this reason renounces to a particular love; as a prostitute is a woman of everybody, this responding to mundane interests, the other for her love to God."[11] Illich clarified that he was using a comparison made by Urs Von Balthasar.[12]

Father del Corro is quoted as saying that "a convent is a mad house, as contrary to nature as is a brothel."[13]

Sister Consuelo Vásquez is quoted as stating that "the feast of Corpus and the exposure of the Blessed Sacrament will disappear with time for Jesus came to become 'nourishment' not to be adored."[14]

The preceding lines show a critique of an institution that in the view of the presenters had lost central Christian principles and its spiritual

---

8 Oficio Catequístico Arquidiocesano, "Informe que su director, Mons. Francisco Aguilera envía al delegado de la sede apostólica sobre el curso de verano que se impartió del 11 julio-19 agosto 1966," in Tarsicio Ocampo, ed., *Mexico: "Entredicho" del Vaticano a CIDOC 1966–1969, CIDOC Dossier*, no. 37 (Cuernavaca, Mexico: CIDOC, 1969), 4/17 and 4/18.

9 Oficio Catequístico Arquidiocesano, "Informe que su director," 4/12 and 4/13.

10 Oficio Catequístico Arquidiocesano, "Informe que su director," 4/19.

11 Oficio Catequístico Arquidiocesano, "Informe que su director," 4/20.

12 Oficio Catequístico Arquidiocesano, "Informe que su director," 4/21.

13 Oficio Catequístico Arquidiocesano, "Informe que su director," 4/25.

14 Oficio Catequístico Arquidiocesano, "Informe que su director," 4/22.

relevance and that had become corrupt. They also show a serious gender bias towards women religious, and they neglect those working under challenging circumstances at the time in various parts of the world, including Central America. The letter to the papal nuncio in Mexico was dated 20 September 1966, and Illich's letter to Pope Paul VI asking for a private audience to explain his work with missionaries to Latin America was dated 29 August 1966. He mentioned in his letter that they would be in Rome from the 15th to the 24th of September to talk to sixty-five Latin American priests.[15]

The statements were made in 1966, a year after the conclusion of the Vatican II Council that led to a renewal of the church and dramatic changes in liturgy and to the relations of the church with other communities of faith and the modern world, as well as to religious congregations having to go back to review their original inspiration. However, the council did not deal with sexuality; the structural, patriarchal, authoritarian character of the church; or the political role of the church. Illich and his colleagues were not concerned with patriarchy but with other oppressive characteristics of religious life, as well as the politics of the church. There was a concern with poverty, as was reflected in the *CIF Reports* from the start, but no reference in the writings to the extensive struggle for civil rights in the United States, Black people's struggle, the situation of Indigenous people in Latin America and their experience and cultures, the women's movement, or in the early 1970s, to the struggles of LGBTQ people.

The articulations of the ideas at the sessions on catechism and in the publications we will discuss reflect the language of psychoanalysis evocative of Erich Fromm's interpretation of Freud, conveyed in a preoccupation with psychological needs, desires, pleasure, and happiness, relief of tensions and physical desires, reason as a tool to establish moral values, an emphasis on awareness, and responsibility for one's own actions.[16] Fromm rejected Freud's as well as Marxist determinism.[17] As we referred to in the previous chapter, the influence of psychoanalysis was powerful in Cuernavaca and led to its open embracement

---

15 Letter from Ivan D. Illich Alla Sua Santita, Papa Paulo VI, Citta del Vaticano, dated Cuernavaca, 29 August 1966, in Tarsicio Ocampo, ed., *Mexico: "Entredicho" del Vaticano a CIDOC 1966–1969, CIDOC Dossier*, no. 37 (Cuernavaca, Mexico: CIDOC, 1969), 4/28.

16 Rosa Bruno-Jofré and Jon Igelmo Zaldívar, "Monsignor Ivan Illich's Critique of the Institutional Church, 1960–1966," *Journal of Ecclesiastical History* 67, no. 3 (July 2016): 568–86, particularly 581.

17 Erich Fromm, *The Heart of Man: Its Genius for Good and Evil* (New York: Harper & Row, 1964), 14–15.

by Lemercier and Méndez Arceo. Fromm, who was a friend of Illich, wrote introductions to his work, contributed to *CIDOC Informa*, and questioned the philosophical frame of reference used by Freud, in particular the mechanistic materialism current among natural scientists at the beginning of the twentieth century, and instead articulated a dialectical humanism as a frame of reference.[18] In this way, Freud's discoveries, such as the Oedipus complex, narcissism, and the death instinct, would become more meaningful and would imply a "blend of relentless criticism, uncompromising realism, and rational faith."[19] According to Fromm, religion was not superego or an internalization of an external authority, but its practice was rooted in the ego, or life force.[20] Prior Lemercier, another influential figure in Cuernavaca discussed in the previous chapter in relation to Méndez Arceo and Illich, pursued a spiritualized psychoanalysis that touched "the deepest nucleus of the personality; there is no interest in a psychoanalysis that leaves the religious spirit untouched while pretending to analyze all other human traits ... This is evidently an act of faith: faith in the religious spirit, faith in science and faith in faith itself."[21] Lemercier explained in 1965 that psychoanalysis did not dissolve religion but transformed it by a process of interiorization.[22] Illich did not discuss the benefits of psychoanalysis in the way Lemercier or Méndez Arceo did; however, it is arguable that "The Seamy Side of Charity" and "The Vanishing Clergyman," two documents critical of the institutional church, reflect the influence of psychoanalysis, among other intertwining intellectual threads.

"The Seamy Side of Charity" was first published in New York in January 1967, in the Jesuit magazine *America*, and was translated into Spanish two months later.[23] It made explicit an anti-imperialist critique of the political alliance of US Catholics with the US project for Latin America, mainly the Alliance for Progress, and a focal point was the 1961 call from John XXIII to religious congregations to send 10 per cent of their

---

18   Lawrence Jacob Friedman, *The Lives of Erich Fromm: Love's Prophet* (New York: Columbia University Press, 2013), 294.

19   Fromm, *The Heart of Man*, 14–15, quotation on 15.

20   Erich Fromm, *Escape from Freedom* (New York: Continuum, 1941).

21   Gregorio Lemercier, "A Benedictine Monastery and Psychoanalysis," in *CIF Reports*, no. iv (1965); reprinted in CIDOC, *CIF Reports*, vol. 4, January–December 1965, *CIDOC Cuaderno*, no. 39 (Cuernavaca, Mexico: CIDOC, 1970), 10/24.

22   Lemercier, "A Benedictine Monastery," 10/24.

23   Ivan Illich, "The Seamy Side of Charity," *America* 116, no. 21 (1967): 88–91; Ivan Illich, "Las sombras de la caridad," *CIDOC Informa*, January–June 1967, no. 67/3, 3/1–3/11. *Esprit* published a version in French entitled "envers de la charité," in March 1967, in its issue 35.

members to Latin America. It was interpreted, Illich said, as a call to help modernize the Latin American church along the lines of the North American model. "The continent on which half of all Catholics live had to be saved from 'Castro-Communism.'"[24] The "red danger" was part of the recruitment literature. By 1966 the project had failed and only 0.7 per cent of the US and Canadian clergy had moved to the south. In the introductory lines to "The Seamy Side of Charity," included in *Celebration of Awareness* (1970), he stated in 1970 that he opposed the church program and mentioned the creation of a centre in Cuernavaca with two friends because he wanted to diminish the damage threatened by the papal order and create awareness in the missionaries so that they could either refuse the assignment or be better prepared. Illich also mentioned that "the transfer of US living standards and expectations could only impede the revolutionary changes needed."[25] However, he neglected to refer to the early financial ties of the United States to the centres, leaving out of his statement his own political manoeuvring at the time and his move to financial independence, in particular with CIDOC.

Central points of the argument are the transplantation of a foreign Christian image, the negative effect of foreign money, people, and ideas, the alliance of the institutional church with US policies and agendas, and the church "becoming an 'official' agency of one kind of progress."[26] Illich was aware of the impact on the Latin American church. By relying on money from the north, it was becoming a satellite of the North American church and returning to what the colony had stamped on her: "a colonial plant that blooms because of foreign cultivation."[27] An interesting comment was included in the critique that seems to be out of line with his future critique of schooling: "Education, the one type of investment that could give long-range returns, is conceived mostly as training for bureaucrats who will maintain the existing apparatus."[28]

Illich, who in his critique does not move to the theological understanding of social justice, made it clear that the church had become an agency trusted to run programs aiming at social change. He wrote, "But when it is threatened by real change, it withdraws rather than permit

---

24 Ivan Illich, "The Seamy Side of Charity" in Ivan Illich, *Celebration of Awareness: A Call for Institutional Revolution* (New York: Doubleday, 1971), 39.

25 Illich, "The Seamy Side of Charity," in *Celebration of Awareness*, 39.

26 Illich, "The Seamy Side of Charity," in *Celebration of Awareness*, 47.

27 Illich, "The Seamy Side of Charity," in *Celebration of Awareness*, 46.

28 Illich, "The Seamy Side of Charity," in *Celebration of Awareness*, 46.

[*sic*] social awareness to spread like wildfire,"[29] giving the example of the Brazilian radio schools smothered by the high church authority. An important point in Illich's critique of the church's engagement with the United States is its involvement in the indoctrination of a way of life that the rich had chosen as suitable for the poor – a certain type of democracy portrayed as the Christian ideal. The church had ceased, Illich said, to speak for the underdog outside of the agencies, but instead represented the majority, and he made a statement with political implications: "By accepting the power to help, the Church necessarily must denounce a Camilo Torres, [the guerrillero priest from Colombia] who symbolizes the power of renunciation. Money thus builds the Church a 'pastoral' structure beyond its means and makes it a political power."[30] Illich denounced the potential damage that foreign priests could cause to the church in Latin America by performing roles that lay people could take on: the situation would mean that there was "no need to re-examine the structure of the parish, the function of the priest, the Sunday obligation and the clerical sermon; no need to explore the use of the married diaconate, new forms of celebration of the Word and Eucharist, and intimate familial celebrations of conversion to the Gospel in the milieu of the home."[31] This is key to his critique of the church, the structure, and the related bureaucracy as well as the hierarchy's unconscious fear of a new church.[32] He had worked on a resignification of the role of the missionary and, in his view, had experienced "real" volunteers – those with a sense of authenticity – who wanted to face the truth that would put their faith to the test.[33]

Illich made explicit an anti-imperialist position. However, he critiqued the structure of the church and its bureaucracy through theological lenses that retained conservative theological traits, while placing the church beyond any ideological struggle. Thus, he questioned the use of the gospel for capitalism and for any other ideology. At the same time, he was clear that, although the Alliance for Progress appeared to be driven by Christian justice, it was a deception aimed at maintaining the status quo.

Illich said, in the introduction he wrote for "The Seamy Side of Charity," included in *Celebration of Awareness*, that he had written the article for the Jesuit magazine *America* in January 1967 because, at the end of

29 Illich, "The Seamy Side of Charity," in *Celebration of Awareness*, 47.
30 Illich, "The Seamy Side of Charity," in *Celebration of Awareness*, 47–8.
31 Illich, "The Seamy Side of Charity," in *Celebration of Awareness*, 49.
32 Illich, "The Seamy Side of Charity," in *Celebration of Awareness*, 50.
33 Illich, "The Seamy Side of Charity," in *Celebration of Awareness*, 51.

January, 3,000 church members – Catholic and Protestant – from the United States and Latin America would meet in Boston to move the programs ahead. Another reason was that the magazine *Ramparts* was about to publish in February an exposé of the CIA penetration of students' organizations.

"The Seamy Side of Charity" generated strong reactions. In March *America* devoted a special section to the response.[34] The special section of 4 March opened with a letter from Chilean Renato Poblete, S.J., a high-profile Jesuit at the time, and seriously questioned recently for his sexual behaviour, although he died in 2010. He had taught in Illich's CIC in Cuernavaca. Poblete questioned Illich's statement that the Latin American church was alienated and that the ecclesiastical bureaucracy cultivated a colonial church. For Poblete, this was an example of overgeneralization that he found ironic, since Illich had made the point again and again that there was no one Latin America. A twisted and narrow interpretation of the text, indeed. Poblete acknowledged the need for constant criticism and self-evaluation (which Illich did not limit to methods and institutions but extended to the institutions they embodied). Poblete tried to make the case that US priests working in the south were not necessarily agents of companies or of the CIA.[35] The church, he argued, had a universal character: "the Church in Latin America [has] received constant influence from different corners of the world. This has enriched, rather than alienated us."[36] Poblete, who did not acknowledge Illich's inspiration in the early years of Christianity, positioned himself politically in a comfortable place within the church, while not capturing Illich's experience in Cuernavaca nor his reading of the time. A number of Latin American theologians and church leaders were already engaged in a critical process of renewal of the church.

Poblete neglected to consider Illich's concern with authenticity informing the missionary vocation of lay and ordained missionaries. Illich was of course influenced by existentialism and by social psychoanalysis and his friend Erich Fromm, as revealed in his aim to unmask institutions, whether they were working for the people or for ideological and economic interests that were not revealed.

Illich had developed a strong anti-imperialist stance that was dominant in Latin American critically minded circles. Here we are talking of the "long 1960s" and the way he approached the critique of the

---

34 Taken from Bruno-Jofré and Igelmo Zaldívar, "Monsignor Ivan Illich's Critique."
35 Renato Poblete, "Religious Imperialism in Latin America?" *America* (4 March 1976).
36 Renato Poblete, "Religious Imperialism in Latin America?" *America* (4 March 1976): 317.

structure of the church by questioning the close political relationship and alliance of sectors of the church with American interests in Latin America. Illich wrote that, "The influx of the United States missioners coincides with the Alliance for Progress, Camelot, and CIA projects and looks like a baptism of all three."[37]

Joseph P. Fitzpatrick, S.J., a sociologist at Fordham University who had worked with Illich in Puerto Rico in the 1950s, wrote an article entitled "What is He Getting At?" that was published on 25 March 1967, in which he explains Illich's ideas within the context of his experience.[38] Fitzpatrick made it clear that it would be unfortunate if the anger and resentment the article created obscured the serious issues it raised. Illich, he said, "has a vision of the radical changes the Church must undergo if it is to be Christ's present to the men [sic] of the 21st century."[39] Fitzpatrick grasped a key point in Illich's critique of missionaries and foreign priests, whose conception of a vigorous church was founded in the mystique of their country of origin. Fitzpatrick wrote: "For years, [Illich] has been pointing to one of the major failures in American apostolic ventures in Latin America, one that desperately needs correcting. He is still pointing to it, but now in a larger context, not only religious but also political and economic. It will be a tragedy if this is brushed off as an expression of his supposed anti-Yankee sentiments or his lack of charity toward American priests."[40]

"The Seamy Side of Charity" conveys Illich's central concerns about missions through the language of the late 1960s, in particular the church hierarchy's understanding of the universality of the church, tainted by the ideological alliance with US politics towards Latin America. The configurational components of the time included psychoanalysis, existentialism, and Sartre's "theory of commitment," anti-war (principally the Vietnam War) protests, a critique of authority and of the predominance of economic over civil interests, liberation of sexuality, a movement towards gender equality, and of course the civil rights movement. A theme that crossed the various discourses was the questioning of highly bureaucratized forms of public and private management. The latter is evident in the countercultural movements of the north in all their variants. The church was seen by Illich as a bureaucratic organization with a structural problem that created distorted intentionalities

---

37 Illich, "The Seamy Side of Charity," in *Celebration of Awareness*, 52.
38 Joseph P. Fitzpatrick, "What is He Getting At?" *America* 116, no. 12 (25 March 1967): 444–8.
39 Fitzpatrick, "What is He Getting At?" 444.
40 Fitzpatrick, "What is He Getting At?" 445.

that were far from the gospel. This is an issue that we find in "The Vanishing Clergyman," published the same year as "The Seamy Side of Charity."

The theme runs powerfully through "The Vanishing Clergyman." The first line reads: "THE ROMAN CHURCH IS THE WORLD'S LARGEST NON-governmental bureaucracy. It employs 1.8 million full-time workers-priests, brothers, sisters, and laymen [sic]."[41] The sharp statements reveal a radicalized Illich. However, as mentioned in another chapter, Illich indicated in the introduction that he drafted this paper in 1959, and this was obviously while he was in Puerto Rico.

Illich fully addressed the changes needed in the structure of the Catholic Church if it were to survive. He wrote in the introductory comments to "The Vanishing Clergyman" in the 1971 edition of *Celebration of Awareness* that these changes could be thought of "in terms consistent with the most radically traditional theology."[42] He developed a thesis on what would happen to the clergyman (*sic*), a disappearing profession, as well as to his role and his community and professional status in light of the continuing growth of the bureaucracy. He expected to render the emerging discussion relevant to the Catholic left, although he did not wish to compromise fundamental traditional positions ("the value of freely chosen celibacy, the episcopal structure of the Church, the permanence of priestly ordination").[43] Although he welcomed the disappearance of the institutional bureaucracy with joy, and he suggested ways in which the church could seek "a radical reorganization in some of its structures,"[44] he did not recommend essential changes in the church, and even less its dissolution. The point here is that the possible changes he outlined were "solidly rooted in the origins of the Church" but reached out to meet the necessities of the world of the day. He wanted a faith that was not mediated by the institution. In his view, the institutional church was in trouble, and he questioned full-time celibacy and foresaw the future of the ministry as being comprised of "ordained laymen" – indeed, not women – able to earn a living outside the church. It meant the ordination of secularly employed men. Without going into organizational details, his notion of diaconia (involvement of lay people in the ministry), his critique of seminaries, and his realistic

---

41 Ivan Illich, "The Vanishing Clergyman," in *Celebration of Awareness: A Call for Institutional Revolution* (New York: Doubleday, 1971), 59. Capitalized words are written as they appear in the original text.

42 Illich, "The Vanishing Clergyman," 57.

43 Illich, "The Vanishing Clergyman," 58.

44 Illich, "The Vanishing Clergyman," 60.

critique of church services as impersonal attendance around the altar, Illich wanted a Christian ministry in a pluralistic and secular society. He paid particular attention to ministry and celibacy. In his view, those religious who abandoned celibacy had thereby gone through a process of purification of their faith. In line with his radical humanist approach and familiarity with psychoanalysis, Illich wrote that when ordained men (sic) understood the sociological, psychological, and mythological reasons for celibacy, they recognized its irrelevance to true Christian renunciation.[45]

Illich went straight to the mechanisms to control evangelical charisma – the social and juridical organization of religious communities, and the vows taken by religious – and made the case that the vows should be a rite to testify one's authenticity after many years of living a secular life of renunciation. This is in line with the statements made by Illich and associates to religious women and men during the summer course in Mexico City in 1966. Beyond the intellectual influence of psychoanalysis, sexuality was an issue that preoccupied Illich and other members of CIDOC, and of course Lemercier and the Benedictine monks at the Monastery Santa María de la Resurrección.

The publication of "The Vanishing Clergyman" marked a break in Illich's joint journey with Méndez Arceo in Cuernavaca, although they continued to be friends. Méndez Arceo wrote to Illich that his critique of the bureaucratic apparatus of the church had become a caricature that ignored the church's tradition – the supernatural dimension of human values behind the structures whose disappearance, not renewal, Illich was advocating in the name of the gospel. Méndez Arceo said that "The Vanishing Clergyman" would lead to discouragement and disillusion. While acknowledging the need for freedom in research as maintained in *Gaudium et Spes*, or Pastoral Constitution on the Church in the Modern World (1965),[46] he wrote that "this freedom has responsibility as counterpart, I must say publicly that (leaving aside the content of the article), this publication in Mexico, the way it was done, it has been a serious error."[47]

---

45 Illich, "The Vanishing Clergyman," 76. Also see Bruno-Jofré and Igelmo Zaldívar "Monsignor Ivan Illich's Critique," 584.

46 Paul VI, *Gaudium et Spes*, Pastoral Constitution on the Church in the Modern World (Vatican: The Holy See, 7 December 1965), http://www.vatican.va /archive/hist_councils/ii_vatican_council/documents/vat-ii_const_ 19651207_gaudium-et-spes_en.html.

47 Sergio Méndez Arceo, 1967, "Carta del Obispo de Cuernavaca a Monseñor Ivan D. Illich," in Baltasar López (comp.), *Cuernavaca: Fuentes Para el Estudio de una Diocesis*, 1959–1968, *CIDOC Dossier*, no. 31 (Cuernavaca, Mexico: CIDOC, 1969), 4/9, 4/10.

In "The Powerless Church" Illich introduces his conception of the function of the church; she has become powerless to produce development, but she can be a celebrant of the mystery. Both the priests making collections to serve the poor and the rebel priest working as agitator are making a living and become an obstacle to the specific function of the church: "the annunciation of the Gospel."[48] There is a paragraph that fully shows Thomas Aquinas's influence – the notion of experience and sensory experience. The reaction of the human heart to change indicates the objective value of that change, and this experience is available "through the celebration of shared experience: dialogue, controversy, play, poetry – in short, self-realization in creative leisure, not tables, plans. The church teaches us to discover the transcendental meaning of this experience of life."[49] She reveals to us the personal responsibility for our sins (agency so relevant in Aquinas's theology), in which Illich includes isolation, growing dependence, self-alienation in things, systems, etc.[50] We can find in the preceding lines elements of the framework of Illich's notion of schooling and education that are not always fully articulated.

In the introduction to *Celebration of Awareness*, Erich Fromm refers to Illich's approach, which certainly varied over time, as humanist radicalism; radicalism refers to an attitude, an "approach" wherein everything must be doubted, "particularly the ideological concepts which are virtually shared by everybody and have consequently assumed the role of indubitable commonsensical axioms."[51] Radical doubt means, in Fromm's words, to question. It is "a process of liberation from idolatrous thinking; a widening of awareness, of imaginative, creative vision of our possibilities and options."[52]

The Reaction to Illich's Critique of the Church as Institution

The participation of Illich and some of his close collaborators in the summer course on catechesis in 1966, mentioned before, and the statements they made had set an alarming stage for the Mexican ecclesiastical authorities who wanted to remove Illich from Mexico. Illich's process of radicalization in his approach to the institutional church

---

48 Ivan Illich, "The Powerless Church," in Ivan Illich, *Celebration of Awareness: A Call for Institutional Revolution* (New York: Doubleday, 1971), 87–94, quotation on 87.

49 Illich, "The Powerless Church," in *Celebration of Awareness*, 89.

50 Illich, "The Powerless Church," in *Celebration of Awareness*, 89.

51 Erich Fromm, "Introduction," in Ivan D. Illich, *Celebration of Awareness. A Call for Institutional Revolution* (New York: Doubleday, 1971), vii.

52 Fromm, "Introduction," viii.

reached a high point with the publication in February 1967 of "The Seamy Side of Charity" and in June of "The Vanishing Clergyman," and the process against Illich began to take shape. After receiving complaints from Mexican bishops, the Episcopal Latin American Conference (CELAM) conducted an onsite inspection from 21 to 24 September 1967. The visiting reviewers made clear to Illich that many of his criticisms of the church were offensive and their publicity sensationalist. Although Illich admitted to the objections regarding the sensationalism generated by publicity, he said his intention was "to inform the public opinion and urge a review of the problems related to the US input in Latin America and those related to the structure of the clerical state."[53] Illich expressed his disposition of fidelity to the church, a statement that he would repeat a few times during the conflict with the Vatican as well. The CIDOC report on the visit said in one of its conclusions that CELAM would have to decide with clarity whether or not it accepted the presence of CIDOC as a civil institution, independent of the ecclesiastical hierarchy.[54] The reviewers recommended dialogue rather than action against Illich and/or CIDOC.[55]

A group of Mexican bishops restarted the campaign to remove Illich from Mexico and force him back to the dioceses of New York where he was registered. On 12 October 1967 he wrote to Cardinal Spellman, his protector, saying:

> The Bishop of Cuernavaca has evidence that you will soon receive a flood of requests that you withdraw me from Mexico. Some may come from Mexican Bishops and perhaps some from Rome.
>
> I take the liberty of reminding your Eminence that in 1966 I bound myself contractually for a five to ten year period to the presidency of CIDOC. My conscience would not allow me to consider violating this contract, because many other people depend on my continued association with this organization. Moreover, this contract is legally binding upon me. I made this contract only after having obtained a corresponding leave of absence from the Archdiocese.

---

53 Lucio Gera, "Informe dirigido al Exmo, Sr. Avelar Brandao Vilela, president of CELAM, sobre la visita que hizo con Mons. Cándido Padim al CIDOC y anexo informe de Valentina Borremans," Roma, 30 September 1967, in Tarsicio Ocampo, ed., *Mexico: "Entredicho" del Vaticano a CIDOC 1966–1969, CIDOC Dossier*, no. 37 (Cuernavaca, Mexico: CIDOC, 1969), 4/33.

54 Gera, "Informe dirigido al Exmo," 4/33. See also Borremans to Candido Padim and Lucio Gera and those listening, Mexico, 25 September 1967, 4/35–4/37.

55 Gera, "Informe dirigido al Exmo," 4/38.

May I venture to suggest to Your Eminence that reference to this contract should be a sufficient explanation of my continuing in my present work to anyone who might request my withdrawal.

I am continuously grateful for Your Eminence's kindness toward me, which I hope will enable me to serve the Church the best I know.[56]

The subsequent letter from Spellman to the archbishop of Puebla makes a strong argument supporting Illich, but it refers to the Centre for Intercultural Formation (CIF) and not to CIDOC (the centre mentioned in Illich's letter to Spellman), as if he were not willing to recognize or acknowledge what Illich was doing. Furthermore, everything Illich was doing was against Spellman's central pastoral discourse, well known in the Catholic Church, particularly after Vatican II, where he represented the most conservative of positions.[57] Spellman's letter is dated 10 November, and he died on 2 December 1967.

In spite of the pressure Mexican conservative leaders put on the Vatican to get Illich out of the country, as Fitzpatrick put it, "nothing happened while Spellman was alive."[58] On 12 December 1967, Illich wrote to Bishop Méndez Arceo to request something he had wanted to for a long time but hadn't out of respect to the late Cardinal Spellman: he resigned from his pontifical honorific titles, including secret waiter for his holiness and monsignor.[59] He wrote that within the context and the specific circumstances in Mexico, it was ambiguous that a priest, and even more so a member of the Pontifical Court with the title of monsignor, would perform academic functions.[60] Illich made the point that he

---

56 Ivan Illich, letter to Cardinal Spellman, Cuernavaca, 12 October 1967, in Tarsicio Ocampo, ed., *Mexico: "Entredicho" del Vaticano a CIDOC 1966–1969*, CIDOC Dossier, no. 37 (Cuernavaca, Mexico: CIDOC, 1969), 4/38.

57 Letter to the Archbishop of Puebla from Cardinal Spellman, *CIDOC Dossier*, no. 37, 4/39. Spellman wrote to the archbishop of Puebla: "As you know the Centre of Intercultural Formation (CIF) is an educational and formation institute, established in cooperation with Fordham University, and is directed by a Board of which the rector of the university is president. The primary centre has been established in Cuernavaca. In 1961, Monsignor Illich was requested by the Board to assume the post of Executive Director of CIF for a period of five years and was granted permission to do so. In early 1966, the board requested that he accept a second five-year term and he was again permitted to do so."

58 Joseph P. Fitzpatrick, *The Stranger Is Our Own: Reflections on the Journey of Puerto Rican Migrants* (Kansas City: Sheed & Ward, 1996), 29.

59 Ivan Illich to Bishop S. Méndez Arceo, Cuernavaca, 12 December 1967, in Tarsicio Ocampo, ed., *Mexico: "Entredicho" del Vaticano a CIDOC 1966–1969*, CIDOC Dossier, no. 37 (Cuernavaca, Mexico: CIDOC, 1969), 4/41.

60 Illich to Méndez Arceo, 12 December 1967, 4/41.

was part of an organization independent from the church's hierarchy and that the titles generated confusion in his circles. The confusion was even greater in ecclesiastical settings, where his condition as clergy and his titles gave an opening to the hierarchy to intervene in the life of the centre. For that reason, he had declined pastoral or ministerial functions.[61] The same day, he wrote to the pope requesting that his name be removed from the list of Chaplain of His Holiness, the title given to him by John XXIII.[62] He was, in other words, fencing with his centre (in Cuernavaca), but not attacking the church as such, and was building some coherence with his critique of the institutional church, the *church as It.*

The death of Spellman, Illich's protector, had an impact on Illich's life. The day after Spellman's burial, the Vatican instructed the administrator of the New York Archdiocese to call Illich back to New York.[63] Of course he did not go back, which was construed as a lack of obedience.[64] At his meeting with the Apostolic delegate Guido del Mestri, Illich reasserted his decision not to leave CIDOC, as it was a moral issue for him, and in his letter to del Mestri after the interview, Illich wrote: "I wish to reiterate to His Excellence what has always been my position regarding the teaching magisterium of the Holy See. Hence, if in any of my writings an erroneous affirmation about our faith would be considered erroneous in the judgement of the Holy See and to my embarrassment, I would like to be told immediately in order to declare, quickly and without discussion, my total submission to the religious authority on that matter."[65]

On 22 January 1968, in a letter addressed to the pope, he explained his situation, referring to the 1966 contract with CIDOC and the serious moral, cultural, and civil responsibilities implied, and he questioned the decision from the Sacred Congregation for the Doctrine of the Faith

---

61 Illich to Méndez Arceo, 12 December 1967, 4/41.
62 Ivan Illich to the Holy Father Paul VI, Cuernavaca, 12 December 1967, in Tarsicio Ocampo, ed., *Mexico: "Entredicho" del Vaticano a CIDOC 1966–1969, CIDOC Dossier,* no. 37 (Cuernavaca, Mexico: CIDOC, 1969), 4/40.
63 Letter of John J. Maguire, Archdiocese of New York, 3 January 1968; Illich to Paul VI, 12 December 1967, 4/45. Maguire referred to the Sacred Congregation for the Doctrine of the Faith's decision of 19 December 1967 and demanded Illich's return to New York by 12 January, at the latest. See Tarsicio Ocampo, ed., *Mexico: "Entredicho" del Vaticano a CIDOC 1966–1969, CIDOC Dossier,* no. 37 (Cuernavaca, Mexico: CIDOC, 1969).
64 Fitzpatrick, *The Stranger Is Our Own,* 29–30.
65 Ivan Illich, letter to the Apostolic Delegate (nuncio), Cuernavaca, 18 January 1968, in Tarsicio Ocampo, ed., *Mexico: "Entredicho" del Vaticano a CIDOC 1966–1969, CIDOC Dossier,* no. 37 (Cuernavaca, Mexico: CIDOC, 1969), 4/62.

to remove him from Cuernavaca without canonical admonition. He made two petitions: a) that if his conduct had not been appropriate, he wanted to know details in order to either retract himself or make the necessary clarification; and b) that in light of the moral and civil commitment he had made, with authorization from the Ordinary (Cardinal Spellman, who had died the month before), which would have been against his conscience to not fulfil, he asked the Holy Father to remove him from his obligations and clerical privileges, if necessary, for the time of his civil contract, but not from celibacy and the prayer of the Holy Office. After fulfilling his civil obligations, he wrote, he expected to petition to return to his ministerial functions.[66] The same day he sent a telegram to the coadjutor archbishop of New York, John Maguire, postponing his trip to New York due to a relapse of Asiatic flu.[67]

Illich was called to Rome for questioning by the Sacred Congregation for the Doctrine of the Faith on 17 June 1968. This is not the place to go into the details of the process, but suffice it to say that Illich decided not to respond to the long inquisitorial questionnaire, and he abandoned his defence.[68] On 24 June 1968 Illich requested by letter that Bishop Méndez Arceo remove the jurisdiction and licences he had received as priest in 1961. That letter gives a clear dimension of his critique from the standpoint of his faith, his vision grounded in the gospel, and the habits of the soul as a Catholic. Two points are worth mentioning here. He wrote to Méndez Arceo:

It was a joy to be able to express faith and love to the universal Church liturgically, something that your episcopal ministry helped me to deepen. Now, however, as I explained in my letter to Cardinal Seper, I cannot publicly represent an authority, a government, and an institution that keep suspicions against me such as those contained or insinuated in the 85 questions that I was given by the judge in the "court" mentioned. For this reason, while there be suspicions, I don't want to have ecclesiastical authority or title or exercise a ministry that wouldn't be common to all the faithful. However, no power will be able to take me from my union in faith with my bishop, because this would mean the exclusion of faith in

---

66 Ivan Illich to the Holy Father, Cuernavaca, 22 January 1968, in Tarsicio Ocampo, ed., *Mexico: "Entredicho" del Vaticano a CIDOC 1966–1969*, CIDOC Dossier, no. 37 (Cuernavaca, Mexico: CIDOC, 1969), 4/63–4/64.

67 Ivan Illich, Cuernavaca, Telegram to John Maguire, New York, 22 January 1968, in Tarsicio Ocampo, ed., *Mexico: "Entredicho" del Vaticano a CIDOC 1966–1969*, CIDOC Dossier, no. 37 (Cuernavaca, Mexico: CIDOC, 1969), 4/65.

68 Igelmo, "Ivan Illich en el CIDOC."

the universal magisterium, to which I submit myself. I will not refuse the con-celebration [to celebrate together] with you, although I will have to abstain from doing that beside you and in liturgical vestment.[69]

On 8 January 1969 the Sacred Congregation sent a letter to Archbishop Méndez Arceo informing him that all Catholic clerics and religious had been forbidden to attend CIDOC, an autonomous academic centre.[70] The prohibition did not work. The letter Illich sent to Méndez Arceo on 14 January 1969, in which he requested his removal ad infinitum from the powers and privileges conferred upon him by the church (from which he had resigned a year earlier for one year), gives a good point of reference to interpret his intentionality in relation to the church. Some points are relevant here: his love of the church (Holy Roman Church) with all her traditions and style had become more tender and profound; with this decision, he complied with his personal vocation, and given the circumstances, he could make a major contribution to the renewal (renovación) of his "beloved Church." He asked for the archbishop's help in the coming years to give testimony of four attitudes: 1) absolute and rigorous submission to the authority of the doctrines established within the church, with its limitations, weaknesses, and anachronisms; he would not work as a theologian and would not allow himself to participate in the translation and adaptation of theological doctrines to our time; 2) love of the church as is because he recognized in her the unique sacramental presence of the Lord among us; 3) acceptance of the canonical laws of the Roman Church; if he would allow himself to act against such laws, he wouldn't like this to be interpreted as a negation on his part of the legislative authority of the church on matters of rites and discipline; 4) his desire to contribute to the profound renewal of the Holy Church. After serving within the structures of the church in various capacities, he believed he could better serve the church's renewal by living a simple life in her presence, with the grace that the Lord was willing to give him.[71] This impressive letter guides us in the interpretation

---

69 Ivan Illich, letter to S. Méndez Arceo, Bishop of Cuernavaca, 24 June 1968, in Tarsicio Ocampo, ed., *Mexico: "Entredicho" del Vaticano a CIDOC 1966–1969, CIDOC Dossier*, no. 37 (Cuernavaca, Mexico: CIDOC, 1969) 4/106–4/108.

70 Cardinal Seper, Sacra Congregatio Pro Doctrina Fidei, Roma, Die 8 Januarii 1969 to Excellentissime ac Reverendissime Domine, in Tarsicio Ocampo, ed., *Mexico: "Entredicho" del Vaticano a CIDOC 1966–1969, CIDOC Dossier*, no. 37 (Cuernavaca, Mexico: CIDOC, 1969), 4/132–4/133.

71 Ivan Illich to the Bishop of Cuernavaca, S. Méndez Arceo, 14 January 1969, in Tarsicio Ocampo, ed., *Mexico: "Entredicho" del Vaticano a CIDOC 1966–1969, CIDOC Dossier*, no. 37 (Cuernavaca, Mexico: CIDOC, 1969), 4/134–4/135.

Figure 3.1. "Basel Fasnachtsbrunnen Jean Tinguely," by Kurt Riedberger, February 2008.

Source: Licensed under CC BY-SA 3.0 (https://creativecommons.org/licenses/by -sa/3.0), via Wikimedia Commons, available from https://en.wikipedia.org/wiki /File:Basel_Fasnachtsbrunnen_Jean_Tinguely.JPG.

of his intentionality at that point but also provides landmarks for the reading of his future work, as we will see. On 15 January Illich wrote to the new archbishop of New York, Terence Cooke, informing him of his irrevocable decision to resign entirely from church service and to renounce totally all of his titles, benefits, and privileges.[72]

Illich decided to publish the medieval inquisitorial questionnaire in *Excélsior*, the Mexican newspaper, on 3 February 1969 and in the *New York Times* on 2 February 1969. It was also published with all the related documentation by CIDOC in a book entitled *México: "Entredicho" del Vaticano a CIDOC 1966–1969*.[73] The questionnaire included questions about a number of people, from Ceslaus Hoinacki (and his marriage to a nun) to Father del Corro and Ms. Oliviere (referred to as a collaborator

---

72 Ivan Illich to the Archbishop of New York, Terence J. Cooke, Cuernavaca, 15 March 1969, in Tarsicio Ocampo, ed., *Mexico: "Entredicho" del Vaticano a CIDOC 1966–1969, CIDOC Dossier*, no. 37 (Cuernavaca, Mexico: CIDOC, 1969), 4/228.

73 Tarsicio Ocampo, ed., *Mexico: "Entredicho" del Vaticano a CIDOC 1966–1969, CIDOC Dossier*, no. 37 (Cuernavaca, Mexico: CIDOC, 1969).

of Camilo Torres) to Francisco Julião and Octavio Paz. The resultant reaction against the Vatican had an international dimension, including a book by two Italian journalists. The Vatican stopped its attacks on Illich; for practical purposes, he was a layman even though he was a priest.

Illich construed the conflict as an issue of internal dissension: the institution was behaving as counter-Gospel. He left the ecclesiastical structures, but not the church. His approach to the bureaucracy of the church was unique. As Edward Fiske wrote in the *New York Times*, Illich's reformist instincts were "coupled with almost medieval orthodoxy on basic dogmatic questions like the nature of the Eucharist."[74]

At CIDOC, he placed his voice in dialogue with the major voices of the time, and his critique moved away from a critique of the church to examine other modern institutions. Illich did not have the protection of Cardinal Spellman any longer, although he kept his contacts. He continued developing his vision of change from his Catholic framework, his concerns with the means to the ends of human action in the Thomist sense, and his belief around the replacement of infused virtues, such as hope, with modernist tools and economic ends.[75]

---

74 Edward B. Fiske, "Illich Goes His Own Way," *New York Times*, Section E, 2 February 1969, 5.
75 Colin Miller, "Ivan Illich, Catholic Theologian (part I)," *Pro Ecclesia: A Journal of Catholic and Evangelical Theology* 26, no. 1 (2017): 373–400.

4 Completing the Journey to *Deschooling Society*: A Radical Critique of Schooling

Contextualizing *Deschooling Society*

The Historical Context of the "Long 1960s" and the Church's Place in It

Illich's critique of the direction of the institutional church, what he would call later the church as It, became an impossible task after the death of Spellman – who had been able to protect him, for reasons we don't know – and in light of the reaction from the Vatican and Illich's response. As we showed in the previous chapter, he maintained his fidelity not only to the church's spirituality but to the doctrine and the magisterium, and, as he stated in some documents, even to the hierarchy. The latter makes it difficult to understand his critique of the church as It unless we interpret his positioning as part of a renewal effort somewhat rooted in an (ill-defined) early church. Illich envisioned the role of the Catholic Church as a spiritual force in society, a point he made clear in "The Powerless Church."[1] However, his understanding of the spirituality of the church remained grounded in a Thomist theology that sustained a hierarchical patriarchal system. We find this to be a major contradiction with his questioning of institutionalization.

As Colin Miller argued, "it is becoming increasingly clear that the best way to understand Illich is the way he understood himself – as a Catholic fiercely loyal to the church and to its traditions, Magisterium, and hierarchy."[2] However, his loyalty, as we explained in the previous chapters, was highly nuanced. Illich's critique of modernity goes all the

---

1 Ivan Illich, "The Powerless Church," *Celebration of Awareness* (New York: Anchor Books, 1971), 85–94.
2 Colin Miller, "Ivan Illich, Catholic Theologian (Part I)," *Pro Ecclesia: A Journal of Catholic and Evangelical Theology* 26, no. 1 (Winter 2017): 81–110, quotation on 81.

way back to his early formation at the Pontifical Gregorian University, and to his familiarity with Thomas Aquinas and with neo-scholasticism as expounded by the Vatican. The church's anti-liberal and anti-modernist positions covered what O'Malley called the "long nineteenth century," going from the French Revolution until the end of the pontificate of Pius XII in 1958.[3] By and large, this long century was characterized by the pre-eminence of the papacy in every area of Catholic life; in this period of the development of the papal teaching authority, the magisterium came to mean the teaching authority of the popes and their congregations.[4] And this was related to definitions of infallibility and papal primacy. In practice, the church and many Catholics had to live in (and carve spaces in) secular states, liberal democracies, and the nation-state. As historian James Chappel argued, a de facto Catholic modernity legitimated alliances between Catholics and others; for example, after the war, European Catholics collaborated with Protestants and liberals with a common cause in mind: a nation-state that defended human rights, religious freedom, European federalism, family values, and a social market economy.[5] As mentioned in chapter 2, Vatican II (1962–5) signified a paradigmatic break on many grounds in the process of "*aggiornamento*," showing the church's adaptation to the modern world without, however, affecting its hierarchical grounding, although the council left Thomism behind. Illich, as discussed earlier, abandoned the council.

It was natural, albeit within the context of his conflict with the Vatican, that Illich redirected his interest away from the complicity of the hierarchy of the church with the US project of modernization of education in Latin America. However, the historical context of the production of *Deschooling Society* contained overlapping configurations of ideas and intentionalities, often in opposition to each other. His critique of modernity became intertwined with his critique of the US-sponsored modernization agenda. Thus, before entering into a discussion of *Deschooling Society*, we will first examine the project to modernize the education system in Latin America in light of its links with economic "development" as part of the US hegemonic project. We will situate this project in a longer view of Latin American political and educational processes. Second, we will discuss the process of secularization and the impact

---

3 John W. O'Malley, *What Happened at Vatican II* (Cambridge, MA: Harvard University Press, 2008), 4.

4 O'Malley, *What Happened at Vatican II*, 4 and 54.

5 James Chappel, *Catholic Modern: The Challenge of Totalitarianism and the Remaking of the Church* (Cambridge, MA: Harvard University Press, 2018), 33.

of pluralism. Third, we will introduce the critiques of education that gained pre-eminence from the late 1950s and whose major protagonists were in close touch with Illich. We will then discuss the three texts we construe as transitional towards *Deschooling Society*: "The Futility of Schooling in Latin America" (1968), "La escuela, esa vieja y gorda vaca sagrada: en América Latina abre un abismo y prepara a una elite y con ella el fascism" (The School, that Old and Fat Sacred Cow: In Latin America It Opens an Abyss between Classes and Prepares an Elite and with Her, Fascism) (1968), and "La metamorfosis de la escuela" (The School's Metamorphosis) (1969). When entering into the discussion of *Deschooling Society*, we will introduce the reader to the publications of what would later be the book, using various avenues, including the *New York Review of Books*. After tracing the journey of the book and how Illich reached the point of writing *Deschooling Society*, the central question will be "what is original about *Deschooling Society*?"

Overlapping Configurations

WHAT WERE THE HISTORICAL CONFIGURATIONS LEADING TOWARDS
THE MODERNIZATION SPONSORED BY THE ALLIANCE FOR PROGRESS?
WHAT OFFENDED ILLICH?
In the early 1960s at the core of the goals of the Alliance for Progress was the modernization of the educational system to focus on the formation of human resources and link schooling to the economy, and a number of international organizations were engaged in the process.[6] Illich had critiqued the church's involvement in the overall project of modernization and its ties with the Alliance for Progress. Illich conceived the latter – as did most Latin American intellectuals and theologians of the time – as imperialistic. The Alliance embodied a counter-revolutionary approach – within the framework of the Cold War – to the influence of the Cuban Revolution, including its successful literacy campaign. The aim was the building of an economic subject, a homo economicus adaptable to the system. As we will see, Latin American historical reality had its own dynamics that intersected with discourses and projects.

---

6 See, for example, the Seminario Interamericano sobre Planeamiento Integral de la Educación held in Washington, DC, in 1958. "Seminario Interamericano sobre Planeamiento Integral de la Educación," *UNESCO Regional Office for the Western Hemisphere (Cuba), Proyecto Principal de Educación UNESCO-América Latina: Boletín trimestral II*, no. 6 (1960).

TO WHAT DID ILLICH REACT AND HOW?

The United States was going through its own crisis in education within the framework of the Cold War, a crisis nourished by the launching of the satellite *Sputnik* into the earth's orbit in 1957 and the public perception of US superiority at the scientific, technical, and military levels. The blame for the perceived lagging behind the Soviets was placed on the US public schools. One of the first policy measures was the National Defense Education Act of 1958.[7] Meanwhile, there was a move in the following decades towards transferring new business management trends to schools, setting the groundwork for the notions of world planning of education and conceiving education as a "quasi-religious promise of salvation" that said people could achieve through schooling by controlling their own destiny.[8] Illich made some acute observations at the time, as we will see. Inequality became quite clear in the long 1960s. It was the time, too, when the notion of meritocracy, coined by Michael Young in his 1958 book *The Rise of the Meritocracy*, became part of the sociological vocabulary, albeit without the original negative connotations. Young described, in a satirical way, a (dystopian) society in which merit that was mostly grounded in intellectual talent, achievement, and success in going through the education system became a central differentiating component – the oligarchy of the future.[9] Thus, Illich's *Deschooling Society* needs to be read contextually since he was attentive to the critiques of modern life emerging at the time.

In a long historical view, Latin American countries had experienced governments that expounded a political nationalist language that was translated into educational reforms. Adriana Puigross places, between 1935 and 1955, pedagogical discourses that were state directed with popular nationalist tones, some being authoritarian, as well as others that emerged from democratic movements. These experiences included Cardenism in Mexico, Peronism in Argentina, Varguism in Brazil, Gaitán's democratic liberalism in Colombia, the Chilean Popular Front with Aguirre Cerda, the Nationalist Revolutionary Movement in Bolivia (including the National Literacy Campaign in 1956), Jacobo Árbenz in

---

7 Wayne Urban, *More than Science and Sputnik: The National Defense Education Act of 1958* (Tuscaloosa: University of Alabama Press, 2010).
8 Anne Rohstock and Daniel Tröhler, "From the Sacred Nation to the Unified Globe: Changing Leitmotifs in Teacher Training in the Western World, 1870–2010," in *Teacher Education in a Transnational World*, ed. Rosa Bruno-Jofré and James Scott Johnston (Toronto: University of Toronto Press, 2014), 111–31, quotation on 126. Illich uses the notion of education as salvation in *Deschooling Society*.
9 Michael Young, *The Rise of the Meritocracy* (London and New York: Routledge, 2017). Originally published in London by Thames and Hudson in 1958.

Guatemala (the Ley Orgánica de Educación of 1952), and the government of Marmaduke Grove in Chile.[10] This model gave way to developmentalist approaches linked to education that were framed by the Alliance for Progress (1961), with its own version and its anti-subversive policy. However, developmentalism, just as any political phenomenon, had various strands and early political expressions. Thus, the form of nationalist developmentalism that took shape in Brazil with support from the Catholic Church in partnership with the state and its radicalization is an interesting example of historical agency and contingency.[11] Joseph Comblin indicates 1956 as a symbolic date, as it was in that year that the bishops who met in Campiña, in northeast Brazil, converged with the agenda of President Juscelino Kubitchek, who founded the Superintendency for the Development of the Northeast (SUDENE), which embodied the collaboration of church and state to support development projects.[12] The work of SUDENE continued with president João Goulart (1961–4), who replaced Jânio Quadros (31 January to 25 August 1961). The broader context of nationalist developmentalism included the peasant movements in northeast Brazil – Francisco Julião being a member of the Brazilian Socialist Party and a major leader in the Communist Party with well-known activist José dos Prazeres – as well as the rapid radicalization of the Basic Education Movement (MEB) sponsored by the bishops, the Movement of Popular Culture, radio schools, cooperatives, etc.[13] Illich was aware of what was

10 Adriana Puigross, *La educación popular en América Latina: Orígenes, polémicas y perspectivas* (Mexico City: Editorial Nueva Imagen, 1984), 26. This is discussed in Rosa Bruno-Jofré, "Popular Education in Latin America in the 1970s and 1980s: Mapping Its Political and Pedagogical Meanings," *Bildungsgeschichte. International Journal for the Historiography of Education* (successor of *Zeitschrift für pädagogische Historiographie*) 1 (2011): 23–39.

11 Alexandre de Freitas Barbose, "'Developmentalist Brazil' (1945–1964) as a Concept: Historicizing and (Re)periodizing Development in Brazil," *Brazilian Journal of Political Economy* 40, no. 2 (April–June 2020): 332–54, Epub 17 April 2020, https://doi.org/10.1590/0101-31572020-3091; Ana Waleska P.C. Mendonça et al., "Pragmatism and Developmentalism in Brazilian Educational Thought in the 1950s/1960," *Studies in Philosophy and Education* 24 (2005): 471–98, https://doi.org/10.1007/s11217-005-1861-8.

12 Joseph Comblin, "La Iglesia Latino Americana desde el Vaticano II," *Contacto X* 15, no. 1 (February 1978); reproduced in ALAI Centre de Doucumentation d'Amerique Latine-SUCO, *Documentación Política*, no. 7, La Tercera Conferencia del CELAM (1) (Montreal, 1978), 119–23; reference is to 121.

13 Andrew Dawson, "A Very Brazilian Experiment: The Base Education Movement, 1961–1967," *History of Education* 85, no. 2 (2002): 185–94; Emmanuel deKadt, *Catholic Radicals in Brazil* (London: Oxford University Press, 1970); Roberto Leher and Paolo Vittoria, "Social Movements and Critical Pedagogy in Brazil: From the Origins of

happening in Brazil and included articles by Marina Bandeira about the MEB in the *CIF Reports* as early as 1962 and by Francisco Julião, leader of the Peasant Leagues, as we discussed in chapter 2. Paulo Freire was part of the picture as well. An active participant in the Movement of Popular Culture in Recife, as first director of the University of Recife's Cultural Extension Program, Freire applied what is now known as the Paulo Freire Literacy Method, which was adopted by MEB and also extended to the entire country as part of the National Literacy Plan. As we discussed before, with the help of Hélder Câmara, Illich had opened CENFI (Intercultural Centre) in 1961 in Anápolis but soon moved to Petrópolis in Brazil to prepare missionaries sent to Brazil following the papal 1961 call, as well as the papal volunteers (PAVLA). The grassroots communities (comunidades eclesiales de base) and even Mass in the vernacular were growing in Brazil as early as 1961.[14]

There were many intersections. Although the US project had national allies and the political and economic influence from international financial institutions was powerful, there was an extended critique of US policies that converged with the left. Grassroots groups questioned the goals and understandings of adult education in particular and started to promote participation, social justice, and transformative approaches. An interesting phenomenon happened between 1968 and 1973: there were attempts at social change with different political connotations, including educational change, by and large with an anti-imperialist tone or a critique of economic dependency, and in some cases with an anti-capitalist slant. These included the national revolution in Peru in 1968, the revolution of General Torres in Bolivia (1970), the return of Perón and the government of Cámpora (1971), and the Popular Unity (Unidad Popular) under Allende in Chile (1970–3), with the latter being the most emblematic. The experience of change in Brazil, within a nationalist developmentalist orientation along with processes of radicalization, ended in 1964 with a coup d'état, and Paulo Freire took refuge in Chile. There he worked until 1969 on projects related to agrarian reform and literacy during the time of the Christian Democratic Party, when important Catholic sectors entered into a process of radicalization.[15] Freire,

---

Popular Education to the Proposal of a Permanent Forum," *The Journal for Critical Education Policy Studies* 13, no. 3 (2015): 145–62.

14 Rosa Bruno-Jofré, "Encountering Social Change at a Time of Rapid Radicalization of the National Church: The Missionary Oblate Sisters in Brazil," *Historical Studies (Canadian Catholic Historical Association)* 85 (2019): 57–72.

15 John D. Hollst, "Paulo Freire in Chile, 1964–1969: Pedagogy of the Oppressed in Its Sociopolitical Economic Context," *Harvard Educational Review* 76, no. 2 (2006): 243–70.

who kept a relationship with Illich and would visit CIDOC, wrote *Pedagogy of the Oppressed* while in Chile (published in Portuguese in 1968 and in English in 1970), a book that embodied his own radicalization. The year 1973 is a marker because of the coup in Chile that led to the experiments with neoliberalism and the privatization of education.

What was in dispute was the ends of educationalization. Education was conceived as a means for social reform, whether it was in a revolutionary context or within a reformist project led by the nation-state with all of its contradictions, or as a means to generate change while avoiding radical turning points and accepting US policies for Latin America. Illich saw the changes within the educational system as an illusionary dead end in his early work. Paulo Freire would critique educational approaches that fomented banking education and propose education as a means for liberation, addressing this in his *Pedagogy of the Oppressed*: "Those truly committed to the cause of liberation can accept neither the mechanistic concept of consciousness as an empty vessel to be filled, nor the use of banking methods of domination (propaganda, slogans – deposits) in the name of liberation."[16] Illich placed himself beyond those alternatives and called for the disestablishment of schooling.

Freire's approach marks a difference with the community education programs, by and large sponsored by the United States, that moved the community to resolve their own problems – without the analysis of the macro and micro situations of injustice and while avoiding the claim for a just order. In this approach, the individual becomes the centre of her/his/their own fate; in Freire's conception of education and adult literacy, the system becomes the centre. Instead, Illich wrote in *Deschooling Society* that one of the main goals for the educational revolution was "to liberate the individual from the obligation to shape his expectations to the services offered for any established profession."[17] In other words, to liberate the individual from schooling and certified teachers.

Of course, missionaries were expected to play a role in community education programs. Illich resignified the understanding of the missionary role in his centre, although he did not support a particular project or liberation theology as Freire did. The point here is that many congregations working in South and Central America (mostly responding over the decade to the papal call of 1961) became critical of educational projects sponsored by the Alliance and were involved in

---

16 Paulo Freire, *Pedagogy of the Oppressed* (New York and London: Continuum, 2005), 79.

17 Illich, *Deschooling Society*, 103.

projects of popular education inspired by liberation theology and Paulo Freire.[18] There was, in other words, a distance between discourse and what actually happened in the field.

Education and economic planning had been on the US agenda since the late 1950s, as Illich experienced in Puerto Rico and learned from his relationship with Everett Reimer; the agenda took on new characteristics towards the end of the 1960s, moving to the notion of crisis of civilization – a defence of the American way of life – a Cold War construction.

There are many antecedents to the efforts articulated by the Alliance for Progress and its ideology, but it suffices to mention the 1958 *Seminario internacional sobre planeamiento integral de la educación* (International Seminar on Integral Educational Planning) held in Washington, DC, in which there was an emphasis on the economy. Meanwhile, UNESCO put great emphasis on education as a factor for economic development, one example being the 1960 UNESCO conference.[19] In 1961 the International Bank for Reconstruction and Development (IBRD) would accept requests for loans of funds to be invested in education and economic development through the Agency for International Development. In 1961, in Punta del Este, Uruguay, the Alliance for Progress was launched. In October 1967, in light of the deterioration of developmentalist projects, President Lyndon B. Johnson sponsored the International Conference on the World Crisis in Education held in Williamsburg, Virginia. The chairperson of the conference, Cornell University president James Perkins, requested that Philip H. Coombs (director of the International Institute for Educational Planning, established by UNESCO in Paris in 1963) set the intellectual framework of the conference.[20] This

---

18   Rosa Bruno-Jofré, *The Sisters of Our Lady of the Missions: From Ultramontane Origins to a New Cosmology* (Toronto: University of Toronto Press, 2020); Rosa Bruno-Jofré and Ana Jofré, "Reading the Lived Experience of Vatican II: Words and Images, The Canadian Province of the Sisters of Our Lady of Missions in Peru," *Historical Studies, Canadian Catholic Association* 81 (Fall 2015): 31–52; Elizabeth Smyth, "From Serving in the Missions at Home to Serving in Latin America: The Post-Vatican II Experience of Canadian Women Religious," in *Catholic Education in the Wake of Vatican II*, ed. Rosa Bruno-Jofré and Jon Igelmo Zaldívar (Toronto: University of Toronto Press, 2017), 153–69.

19   "International Colloquium on Educational Planning and Its Economic and Social Factors," organized by the Institute for the Study of Economic and Social Development, University of Paris, the French National Commission for UNESCO, and UNESCO, Paris, 1959; International Seminar on Educational Reform, Prague, 1959.

20   Philip H. Coombs, *The World Educational Crisis: A Systems Analysis* (Oxford: Oxford University Press, 1968), vi. This book was very popular in comparative education courses.

was a very influential conference that conceptualized education as a system subject to system analysis within an economistic and universalist approach. Of course, the solution was to improve "manpower," to raise the quality of education, efficiency, and productivity.[21] Within Illich's framework, this approach shaped practical and intellectual habits – in St. Thomas dispositions – that were contrary to the gospel because they would determine, as in the case of modernization through education, what we are able to think even about God because tools as mediums affect the subject.[22]

As Illich said in "The Seamy Side of Charity," the church, by collaborating in the modernization endeavour led by the United States with its developmentalist conception of progress, became an "'official' agency of one kind of progress."[23] The planning of education acquired an external intentionality and responded to international interests linked to the economy in spite of the taint of neutrality. Illich's reaction was as much political as theological since within his Thomistic framework the project would be understood as a "coercive necessity," which was not acceptable to him.[24]

It was not an issue of modernity in the sense of what the church fought in the long nineteenth century, although Illich kept elements of that long view. Important virtues such as hope, faith, and love – habits of the soul directed towards the love of God and neighbour – had been replaced in modern times and in a dramatic way in the program of modernization by planning, expectation, and charity, but for Illich, they were counterfeits.[25] Illich did not develop a critical reading of Thomas Aquinas, who incorporated the Aristotelian position of the inferior human natures of slaves and freeborn women into Christian theology. As Lea Boutin in her analysis of patriarchy wrote: "This theology has legitimized racism, colonialism, classism, and sexism in society and Church."[26]

21 Coombs, *World Educational Crisis*, 5.
22 Colin Miller, "Ivan Illich, Catholic Theologian (Part I)," *Pro-Ecclesia; A Journal of Catholic and Evangelical Theology* 26, no. 1 (Winter 2017): 81–110, reference to 83; St. Thomas Aquinas, *The Summa Theologica* (Benziger Bros., 1947 ed.), translated by Fathers of the English Dominican Province, "Treatise on Habits," (Questions 49–54).
23 Ivan Illich, "The Seamy Side of Charity," in *Celebration of Awareness: A Call for Institutional Revolution* (Garden City, NY: Anchor Books, 1971), 47.
24 St. Thomas Aquinas, *The Summa Theologica*, "Part I, Question 82," https://www.ccel.org/a/aquinas/summa/home.html.
25 Miller, "Ivan Illich, Catholic Theologian," 83.
26 Sr. Lea Boutin, MO, *The Women in the Church* (Aurora, ON: Southdown, 1991), 11.

Secularization and Pluralism

Illich was well aware of the decline in church commitment by ordinary people, whether in the traditional Protestant churches or in the Catholic Church, but also of the drastic decline in vocations.[27] He interpreted the lack of vocations as a problem related to corrupted values, in that the church and the capitalist system generated an unhealthy system of values that led to alienation and neurosis: "a healthy sense of values empties the seminaries and the ranks of the clergy much more effectively than does a lack of discipline and generosity." He questioned the recruitment practices in which "bishops become tempted to organize safaris, and hunt out foreign priests and funds for constructing such anomalies as minor seminaries."[28] Women congregations, although Illich does not address them, experienced a steady decline, and many began to reflect on the interplay of gender, gospel, and culture in the post-colonial context. Most vocations in international congregations would start coming from Africa and Asia, having more conservative views on faith and morality while being more supernaturalist.[29] Feminist theology started to become known, and its questioning of persistent dualism, authoritarian obedience, and the exclusive structures of the church, and would move towards a theology that considered the intersection of gender, class, and race, and the environment a bit later.[30]

At the time of Illich's writings in the late 1960s and in 1970–1, the Western world, mainly in Europe, North America, and Australasia, had entered into a process of secularization of consciousness amid increasing plurality; religion was no longer the referent for personal or national identity.[31] But the explosion of the Evangelical movement, strong in the

---

27 Helen Rose Ebaugh, "The Growth and Decline of Catholic Religious Orders of Women Worldwide: The Impact of Women's Opportunity Structures," *Journal for the Scientific Study of Religion* 2, no. 1: 68–75.

28 Illich, "The Seamy Side of Charity," 50.

29 Rosa Bruno-Jofré, "Church, Religion and Morality," in *A Cultural History of Education in the Modern Age*, ed. Judith Hartford and Thomas O'Donoghue (London: Bloomsbury, 2020), 13–34.

30 Some early works are Mary Daly, *Beyond God the Father: Toward a Philosophy of Women's Liberation* (Boston: Beacon Press, 1973); Rosemary Radford Ruether, *Religion and Sexism: Images of Women in Jewish and Christian Traditions* (New York: Simon and Schuster, 1974); and Sandra Schneiders, *Women and the Word* (New York: Paulist Press, 1986). One of the most recent and influential works, a product of many years of commitment to the issue, is Elisabeth Schüssler Fiorenza, *Congress of Wo/men. Religion, Gender, and Kyriarchal Power* (Indianapolis: Dogyear Publishing, 2016).

31 Hugh McLeod, *The Religious Crisis of the 1960s* (Oxford: Oxford University Press, 2007); Callum F. Brown, "What Was the Religious Crisis of the 1960s?" *Journal of Religious History* 34, no. 4 (December 2010): 468–79.

United States in its various expressions and in the Americas, was a concern for the Catholic hierarchy. We can assume that a point of reference in Illich's critique was the loss of the cultural and social hegemony of the Catholic Church and the inability to permeate society with its original values and virtues – that incidentally he denounced – that had been left aside by the hierarchy of the church. Meanwhile, the Episcopal Latin American Conference (CELAM) at the 1968 conference in Medellín, Colombia, produced the Medellín document, a reading of Vatican II (1962–5) through the eyes of a suffering Latin America and a radicalized reading of the conclusions of the Council.[32] It was an influential document in Latin America that legitimized liberation theology. Many congregations across the world tried to convey a commitment to the poor and worked on projects geared to the transformation of society. Illich did not engage with this vision of the church.[33]

The educational landscape exhibited multifarious developments, some introduced in previous paragraphs. By 1970 there was a clear process of scientification of education and a move away from behaviourism to cognitive psychology, focusing on mental activity and the processing of information. In the 1960s some progressive pedagogical practices were moved to the mainstream in North America for a short time (for example, open classrooms). The influence of all these developments reached the Global South and its educational planning.

Parallel to the critiques of schooling and developments in the educational system, Paulo Freire's ideas emerging from practice that were published in the 1960s (*Pedagogy of the Oppressed* was published in Portuguese in 1968) spread all over. Freire's work would inspire the popular education movement in Latin America in the 1970s and 1980s, and his method and ideas were eclectically mixed with various leftist ideologies. His vision of education expounded in *Pedagogy of the Oppressed* was grounded to an important extent in liberation theology, Emmanuel Mounier's personalism, existentialism, dialectical materialism, and Gramscian notions of ideology. The popular education movement remained outside the formal educational system. Freire, nonetheless, influenced educational reforms of various kinds from very early on; of pertinence here is the one in Peru during the Peruvian Revolution proclaimed by Juan Velasco Alvarado (1968–75). The architect of educational reform in Peru in 1972 was Augusto Salazar Bondy, active in CIDOC and a

---

32 See François Houtard, "L'histoire du CELAM ou l'oubli des origines [The History of CELAM or the Forgotten Origins]," *Archives de sciences sociales des religions* 62, no. 1 (1986): 93–105, https://doi.org/10.3406/assr.1986.2404.

33 See Michael Dodson, "Theology and Christian Radicalism in Contemporary Latin America," *Journal of Latin American Studies* 11, no. 1 (May 1979): 203–22.

friend of Illich, who adopted and adapted Paulo Freire's method, including the concept of conscientization, and sought an authentic education based in communities.

Illich attracted to Cuernavaca major figures of the time who were protagonists of transformational and radical change. CIDOC was an ebullient space, a place of convergence of international leaders, intellectuals, theologians, and pedagogues, including Paulo Freire and educational critics such as Paul Goodman, Everett Reimer, John Holt, and Augusto Salazar Bondy, to mention a few. As David Cayley has said, "CIDOC was one of the epicenters of the intellectual ferment of the late 1960s and early 1970s."[34] There was a sense of globalism that informed the 1960s radicalism that permeated the United States, Europe, and the Global South. There was also a sense of the malaise of urbanization, proletarianization, and so on that was generated by changes in the capitalist structure, including the extensive processes of industrialization in the south. The approach to radical change, which certainly was not uniform, was different from previous ones. In fact, "Third Worldism, the ubiquity of the guerrilla, whether in Cuba or Vietnam, the colonial wars, and post-colonial Africa displaced the Eurocentric approach to radical change, and the 'other' entered into the picture with a different spatial sense and a new revolutionary internationalism."[35] There was an emerging new ethical framework underlying multidirectional changes and claims from second-wave feminism and civil rights as well as Indigenous movements. Illich moved to a critique of education and the monopolizing of education by schooling and questioned what he called the mythologizing of education.

The Critique of Schooling in the 1950s and 1960s

Illich's writing on education signified a shift from the critique of the church as institution, as It, to a critique of schooling that used the church as an analogy. In the same way that he wanted to liberate faith from the mediation of the institution, he wanted to liberate education from schooling. The critique of schools and their function was in the air, as it had also become a topic in the seminar organized by

---

34 David Cayley, *Ivan Illich in Conversation* (Toronto: Anansi, 1992), 14.
35 Rosa Bruno-Jofré, "The 'Long 1960s' in a Global Arena of Contention: Re-defining Assumptions of Self, Morality, Race, Gender and Justice, and Questioning Education," *Espacio, Tiempo y Educación* 6, no. 1 (2019): 5–27, quotation on 9. The analysis relied on Michael Watts, "1968 and all that … ," *Progress in Human Geography* 25, no. 2: 157–88, in particular 170.

CIDOC in 1968. It was a time when social historians took a hard look at schooling. Michael Katz, for example, who moved to OISE (Ontario Institute for Studies in Education) in Toronto, Canada, because of his opposition to the Vietnam War, wrote *The Irony of Early School Reform* in 1968 and *Class, Bureaucracy, and Schools: The Illusion of Educational Change in America* in 1971.[36] Katz questioned the triumphant, unilinear, whiggish historical account of the history of education and interpreted the educational system as one that reproduced inequality, as it did not cover the needs of minorities and the poor; he was also critical of the dominant liberal interpretation of the history of compulsory schooling. The main question of the time was: what interests does the school serve? The launching of *Sputnik* in 1957 had created a sense of crisis, causing the ruling class in the United States to embrace a functionalist, efficiency-oriented approach in contraposition to a progressive pedagogy. The Cold War, which had always been conceived of as a cultural war, became even more entrenched in the vision and goals of education.

Denouncing the educational system was not new. In 1956 Paul Goodman, a voice of the counterculture and the New Left, published *Growing Up Absurd*, in which he questioned a canned culture and a system that did not deal with the needs of young people in their process of maturation.[37] In *Compulsory Mis-education* (1964) Goodman questioned the public school in the United States and with it compulsory attendance and related social values that encouraged conformity and the acceptance of corporate needs.[38] He argued that social values had to be changed for the school to change. Goodman, as Illich would be later, was critical of programmed instruction. The two were close friends. Illich said, "during the last part of his life he would spend considerable time with me in Cuernavaca. I consider Goodman one of the greater thinkers I've known, and also a tender, touching person."[39]

Another critic of schooling, Jonathan Kozol, received the National Book Award for *Death at an Early Age: The Destruction of the Hearts and Minds of Negro Children in the Boston Public Schools*, a life history in a

---

36 Michael Katz, *The Irony of Early School Reform: Educational Innovation in Mid-Nineteenth Century Massachusetts* (New York: Teachers College Press, 2001 [1968]); Michael Katz, *Class, Bureaucracy and Schools: The Illusion of Educational Change in America* (New York: Praeger, 1971; revised ed., 1975).

37 Paul Goodman, *Growing Up Absurd: Problems of Youth in the Organized Society* (New York: Random House, 1960).

38 Paul Goodman, *Compulsory Mis-education* (New York: Horizon Press, 1964).

39 Cayley, *Ivan Illich in Conversation*, 201.

ghetto, published in 1967.[40] In 1972 he published *Free Schools*, in which he proposed schools outside of the public education apparatus and the white people's counterculture and advocated for direct contact to meet the needs of those among the poor, the Black, and the dispossessed who had been victimized by the public system.[41]

Re-examining Illich's First Attempts at Critiquing Educational Institutions in the Late 1960s

There was a transition to *Deschooling Society* starting in 1968, as mentioned before, with three texts published after Spellman's death in which Illich used an analogy of the church as It to critique schools. The first of these transitional works from Illich was "The Futility of Schooling in Latin America," published in *Saturday Review* in April 1968, which questioned the role of schools as an institutional model based on meritocracy in the movement towards "progress," a model that served a modern middle class rather than the Latin American urban proletariat and landless rural masses. He also again brought up the question of the transplantation of people and institutions – raised in "The Seamy Side" – because it left little space for creative local solutions.[42]

The second text we identify as transitional is "La escuela, esa vieja y gorda vaca sagrada: En América Latina abre un abismo y prepara a una elite y con ella el fascism" (The School, that Old and Fat Sacred Cow: In Latin America It Opens an Abyss between Classes and Prepares an Elite and with Her, Fascism), published in August 1968 in the Mexican magazine *Siempre*.[43] This text contains Illich's conclusions from a series of international seminars delivered at CIDOC in which missionaries took part. He asserted that "the fundamental reason for the increasing alienation of the marginalized majorities is the progressive acceptance of the 'liberal myth': the conviction that the schools are the panacea for social integration." He went on to write: "Rooted in a tradition, already solid during the time of the encyclopedists, the western man [*sic*] conceives the citizen as a being who went to school. Attending class replaced

---

40 Jonathan Kozol, *Death at an Early Age: The Destruction of the Hearts and Minds of Negro Children in the Boston Public Schools* (New York: Bantam Books, 1967).
41 Jonathan Kozol, *Free Schools* (Boston: Bantam Books, 1972), 17.
42 Ivan Illich, "The Futility of Schooling in Latin America," *Saturday Review*, 20 April 1968, 57–9 and 74–5.
43 Ivan Illich, "La escuela, esa vieja y gorda vaca sagrada: En América Latina abre un abismo de clases y prepara a una elite y con ella el fascismo" (Cuernavaca, Mexico: CIDOC, 1968), 68/95. Originally published in *Siempre* Mexico, D. F., 78 (789), 7 August 1968. Translation by the authors.

the traditional reverence to the priest. The conversion to the nation by means of school indoctrination, replaced the incorporation to the colony by means of the catechesis."[44] His critique targeted the liberal left, which advocated the increase of funding for schooling.[45] In the same way that faith is more than the Catholic institution, he saw education as more than schooling. He developed an anti-modernist argument against schooling society (what has been referred to as the education-alization of society) and argued that the idea of universal literacy was useful to declare education the exclusive competence of schools. His argument has parallels with his critique of the church as It. In his argument, the subjects (learners) attending school appear exhausted, subsumed in the external forces conditioning their lives. The student is a dehistoricized subject, as history is written out of the individual and collective self – outside a history of resistance, the recreation of meanings, and struggles. He did not envision the school as She, as he did with the church. However, Illich stressed in his article "La escuela, esa vaca sagrada" (The School, that Sacred Cow) that human experience should be at the centre of societal development. For that, he said, we need to distinguish between instruction (programmed socialization) and the opening of the consciousness of each individual – a concept close to the notion of conscientization used in Brazil in the early 1960s in popular literacy programs to describe a process of social awareness. In fact, Illich mentioned Paulo Freire's literacy method and his theory of conscientization in this text as an example of a non-structured pedagogical process that enables individuals to know about themselves and their circumstances.

Illich's argument against the monopolization of education by schools and their role to keep the status quo – continued in *Deschooling Society* – has many dimensions and contains pre-modern references that can be read as a critique of the secular formation of the nation-state, an echo of his early neo-medievalist views. It is an argument grounded in a binary logic and positions taken by the church before the Second World War, which is not easy to disentangle.[46]

In the third text, "La metamorfosis de la escuela" (The School's Metamorphosis), Illich's message at the graduation ceremony at the Universidad de Puerto Rico, Río Piedras Campus, on 6 June 1969, he refers to the crisis of the school and the end of the schooling age. He talked of the

---

44 Illich, "La Escuela," 95/3.
45 Illich, "La Escuela," 95/3.
46 James Chappel, *Catholic Modern: The Challenge of Totalitarianism and the Remaking of the Church* (Cambridge, MA: Harvard University Press, 2018), 23.

age of schooling in the same way, he said, that he could talk of the feudal age or of the period of Christianity. Schooling as a means to become useful members of society was a myth, in his view, and he denounced the social unfairness of the system while questioning the meritocratic system of degrees. The speech contains a sharp critique of schooling as a source of inequality and alienation from reality. The students' critique of teachers was, he said, similar to the critique their grandparents had of the clergy. Thus, the deschooling of education and the demythologization of the school had as its analogy the demythologization of the church.[47] The text is a manifesto against indoctrination, and Illich advocates for the space for the individual to invent herself and for the church to have a prophetic role, albeit within a patriarchal framework. Illich is actually questioning "traditional" education in schools and its paradigm.

Deschooling Society: A Critique of Institutionalized Learning and Institutionalized Values

The Publication of Deschooling Society: *An Unusual Process and Unexpected Title*

The first draft of *Deschooling Society* was published in Mexico in September 1970, in the collection *CIDOC Cuadernos* (CIDOC Notebooks) under the title *The Dawn of Epimethean Man and Other Essays*,[48] a title that suggests Illich's questioning of modernity. The volume contained most of the chapters of what would be published in a few months by Harper & Row with the impactful title *Deschooling Society*. Why the change of title? At an encounter in Ginebra in September 1975, in which also Paulo Freire participated, Illich related that Cass Canfield, from Harper & Row, had found the line somewhere in the book and said to him: "Ivan, this is a marvellous title for the book. Let us call it *Deschooling Education*."[49] Illich continued, saying "five years ago I did not have enough sensibility and clarity to say: No, No, we are not talking of the deschooling process, of the particular process in this organization through which education is now elaborated, but we talk about the

---

47 Ivan Illich, "La metamorphosis de la escuela: Mensaje en ocasión de la graduación celebrada en el recinto Universitario de Río Piedras, Puerto Rico," *El Día*, Mexico, 2 July 1969, 10; reprinted in *CIDOC Cuaderno*, no. 44 (Cuernavaca, Mexico: CIDOC, November 1969), 148/1–148/10/.

48 Ivan Illich, *The Dawn of Epimethean Man and Other Essays*, *CIDOC Cuaderno*, no. 54 (Cuernavaca, Mexico: CIDOC, 1970).

49 Paulo Freire, *Ivan Illich: La educación* (Buenos Aires: Galerna, 2002), 42.

society transforming itself in such a way that that process is not necessary any longer."[50] *The Dawn of Epimethean Man* was translated into Spanish in *CIDOC Cuaderno* no. 65 and was titled *Hacia el fin de la era escolar* (Towards the End of the Schooling Era). The book was a commercial success and was translated into many languages.[51]

These chapters of *Deschooling Society* gathered many of the ideas that were at the core of the texts published in 1968 and that are discussed above, although Illich further elaborated on them and published versions of what would later be chapters of the book. As Illich indicated in the introduction to *Deschooling Society*, he had submitted the various parts of the book on Wednesday mornings to the participants in CIDOC programs during the spring and summer of 1970. He received suggestions, comments, and critiques. Illich advised the reader that many would recognize in the pages the ideas of Paulo Freire, Peter Berger, and José María Bulnes Aldunate, as well as Joseph Fitzpatrick, John Holt, Angel Quintero, Layman Allen, Fred Goodman, Gerhard Ladner, Didier Piveteu, Joel Spring, Augusto Salazar Bondy, and Dennis Sullivan. Paul Goodman, Illich wrote, pushed him to revise his thinking, while Robert Silvers provided editorial assistance for chapters 1, 3, and 6. There is a special reference in the introduction to Everett Reimer, with whom Illich was conducting joint research, and at one point the two decided to publish separate books. Everett Reimer published *School is Dead* in 1971.[52] It addresses similar issues to *Deschooling Society*: school is denounced for its elitist tendencies, authoritarian and bureaucratic nature, coercive tendencies, and for treating students and knowledge as if they can be processed – the way the technological world treats everything. Reimer wanted to free education from the schools and made the case for educational networks that would free people from compulsory schooling, moving responsibility to the student herself. He advocated a true education capable of mastering technology rather than being enslaved by it – the latter being a technology that could kill by destroying the environment, creating weaponry, and over-populating. These were the themes of CIDOC. Illich gave them his own twist.

The introductory comments written by Illich show a powerful network of social and educational critics without any women, except for

---

50 Freire, *Ivan Illich*, 42.
51 *La sociedad descolarizada* was published by Barral Editores in 1974. Barral also published *Tools for Conviviality* in 1975; *Energy and Equity* in 1974; and *Medical Némesis* in 1975.
52 Everett Reimer, *School is Dead* (New York: Doubleday & Co, 1971).

Valentina Borremans, who was very close to Illich; the volumes of *CIDOC Documenta*, entitled *Alternatives in Education*, include only one article by a woman, Maxine Greene, a major progressive figure in philosophy of education. The social network analysis of the CIDOC network by Lemmerer counts a small number of women with various levels of connection to other people related to CIDOC or only to Illich at one point in time or another, such as Marion Boyars, Dorothy Dohen, Susan Sontag, Francine du Plessis, and Roslyn Linheim.[53]

In the spring of 1971, *Deschooling Society* was published in New York. The book contained seven chapters: "Why We Must Disestablish Schools," "Phenomenology of School," "Ritualization of Progress," "Institutional Spectrum," "Irrational Consistencies," "Learning Webs," and "Rebirth of Epimethean Man."[54]

Chapter 1, "Why We Must Disestablish Schools," was first published in the *New York Review of Books* under the title "Why We Must Abolish Schooling." It was originally presented at CIDOC in the cycle of seminars in March 1970 and addresses by and large an American audience. It was also published in English in *CIDOC Informa* no. 22 and included in the first volume of the series *Alternatives in Education*, in *CIDOC Cuaderno* no. 75. The first translation into Spanish appeared in volume 71/271 of *CIDOC Cuaderno* and was titled "Por qué debemos privar de apoyo social a las escuelas?" (Why Should We Deny Social Support to Schools?).

Chapter 2, "Phenomenology of School," was the first of the presentations Illich made at Yale University, in New Haven, Connecticut, on 16, 17, and 18 February 1970.[55] These papers were published in the series *CIDOC Sondeos* no. 77 and were included in the book *Ensayos sobre la transcendencia* (*Essays on Transcendence*).[56] Illich indicated that Hanna Steger, Fred Goodman, Paul Goodman, and Peter Berger would be recognized in the text because of the conversations they had.[57]

Chapter 3, "Ritualization of Progress," had been presented at the conference called "Technology: Social Goals and Cultural Options"

53 Elisabeth Lemmerer, *A Social Network Analysis of the CIDOC Network: Examining a Sample of the American-Mexican Scientific Cooperation in the 1960s* (Germany: VDM Verlag Dr. Müller, 2010).

54 Ivan Illich, *Deschooling Society* (New York: Harper & Row, 1971).

55 Ivan Illich, *The Dawn of Epimethean Man and Other Essays*, *CIDOC Cuaderno*, no. 54 (Cuernavaca, Mexico: CIDOC, 1970), 4.

56 Ivan Illich, *Ensayos sobre la Transcendencia*, *CIDOC Sondeos* no. 77 (Cuernavaca, Mexico: CIDOC, 1971).

57 Illich, *The Dawn of Epimethean Man*, 4.

that took place in Aspen, Colorado, from 23 August to 3 September 1970, sponsored by the International Association for Cultural Freedom and the Aspen Institute for Humanistic Studies.[58] The original title in English was "Schooling: The Ritual of Progress" when it was published in the *New York Review of Books*. As per Illich, he rewrote the text after an intense discussion with Everett Reimer and Jordan Bishop. *CIDOC Informa* published the French translation with the title "Pour en finir avec la religion de l'école" (To Put an End to the Religion of School). The version in Spanish was published in *CIDOC Informa* no. 71/323, under the title "Contra la religión escolar" (Against the Religion of Schooling). The final version was published in the series *CIDOC Documenta*, in the collection *Alternatives in Education*, under no. 75.

Chapter 4, "Institutional Spectrum," was the result of a debate Illich had at CIDOC with Valentina Borremans and José María Bulnes Aldunate. The original text was the platform for a six-week seminar at CIDOC, Cuernavaca. The final version owed a great deal to the critical comments of the participants, and, in addition, Illich worked for a week on this text with Everett Reimer and Dennis Sullivan.[59]

Chapter 5, "Irrational Consistencies," was originally presented at the annual meeting of the American Educational Research Association in New York on 6 February 1971. It was also published in the collection *Alternatives in Education*, in the series *CIDOC Documenta*, *CIDOC Cuaderno*, no. 76.

Chapter 6, "Learning Webs," uses as its framework ideas that were discussed at the seminar "Alternatives in Education," directed by Reimer; in fact, Illich said that it was Reimer who wrote the outline of the piece. The final version as it appeared in *Deschooling Society* was published in a special supplement on education in the *New York Times Review of Books*, on 7 January 1971, under the title "Education without School: How It Can Be Done."

Chapter 7, the last chapter, is "Rebirth of the Epimethean Man" and was the result of two open debates with Erich Fromm and Johann Seb. The foundational ideas were the product of a discussion with Valentina Borremans over oral traditions, using materials Illich had brought from Africa. The text was presented in the summer of 1970 as part of a seminar organized to celebrate Fromm's seventieth birthday. The paper was published in the collection *Alternatives in Education*, in the series *CIDOC Documenta*, no. 75 of *CIDOC Cuaderno*.

---

58 Illich, *The Dawn of Epimethean Man*, 4.
59 Illich, *The Dawn of Epimethean Man*, 4.

Going through Issues in the Book

The topic was not unique, and neither were the radical critiques of education in the North American context of the "long 1960s" or of education in the context of the project to modernize Latin America that had been steered by the Alliance for Progress. However, Illich brought a theological dimension to the issues and his own positioning vis-à-vis the state, as well as his resistance to engaging with a political project or vision. This is understandable, given his intellectual and personal history. The church's long critique of modernity became one strand of his background theoretical frame and sustained his analysis, as did his Thomist idea of agency and sensory experience that was enriched by his exposure to Freire's practices; but he moved further to a critique of the institutionalization of learning and the need to disestablish schooling, particularly in *Deschooling Society*.

Intellectually, Illich was influenced by Jacques Maritain, with whom he had a close intellectual relationship, in particular regarding the anti-statist elements of the Catholic tradition for a new age. As Chappel wrote, "Maritain agreed with [Georg] Moenius that a natural political order would be deeply federal and pluralist, respecting natural hierarchies and local power structures instead of sucking them into the maw of the centralizing state."[60] It was a project of federalist anti-capitalism and an anti-modern form of politics. This overall view is reflected in Illich's work, albeit in a hybrid and eclectic way, and it encompasses his critique of the institutionalized church – the church as It – and of schooling in the modern state.

The book is an indictment of schooling, not only as an institution but as an ethos – in other words, as a dominant cultural model that monopolizes education. "Not only education but social reality itself has become schooled," he wrote, and this leads to the institutionalization of values and the modernization of poverty through the hidden curricula of the school.[61] Why? He argued that both the rich and poor depend on schools and hospitals to guide their lives, to define for them what is legitimate and what is not.[62] Schools discourage and disable the poor, keeping them from taking control of their learning.[63] The modernization of poverty is, in his view, at the root of contemporary underdevelopment.[64]

---

60 James Chappel, *Catholic Modern: The Challenge of Totalitarianism and the Remaking of the Church* (Cambridge, MA: Harvard University Press, 2018), 36.
61 Illich, *Deschooling Society*, 2.
62 Illich, *Deschooling Society*, 2.
63 Illich, *Deschooling Society*, 8.
64 Illich, *Deschooling Society*, 3.

Illich pointed out that the United States is showing that no matter how rich a country is, it cannot afford a school system that can meet the demands the system itself creates.[65] Schooling like this, he said, is economically unfeasible, and obligatory schooling polarizes society, reproducing inequality. Moreover, "countries are rated like castes whose educational dignity is determined by the average of school years of its citizens."[66] He made a critical statement on the project to restructure Latin American society using education as a means to increase equality and decrease discrimination. This criticism is grounded in his claim that the myth of schooling justifies the privileges of a select few, but there is no difference between those who claim status through heritage and those who claim their status based on a degree. Scarcity is predicated on the value of licences and degrees, including those of skilled teachers.[67] It is interesting that Michael Sandel, author of *The Tyranny of Merit*, argued in his explanation of the emergence of populism (re: the election of Donald Trump) that "income inequality is now so widespread that the promise of upward mobility is no longer an adequate response." He tied this situation to the problem of "'meritocratic hubris,' the sense that winners and losers are both deserving of their status."[68] Those who are successful are encouraged to feel that success is the consequence of their own doing. Illich envisioned many of the points made by Sandel.

In Illich's perceptive insights, instruction was packed with certification, and social roles were "melted" into schooling. Illich in a unique way used the analogy with the church to explain his points. "School has become the world religion of a modernized proletariat and makes futile promises of salvation to the poor of the technological age. The nation-state has adopted it, drafting all citizens into a graded curriculum leading to sequential diplomas not unlike the initiation rituals and hieratic promotions of former times."[69]

---

65 Illich, *Deschooling Society*, 9.
66 Illich, *Deschooling Society*, 9.
67 Illich, *Deschooling Society*, 15. At this point, he had not developed the notion of scarcity as he did later on, influenced by Karl Polany. See Ivan Illich, *In the Mirror of the Past: Lectures and Addresses, 1978–1990* (New York and London: Marion Boyars, 1992), http://debate.uvm.edu/asnider/Ivan_Illich/Ivan%20Illich_%20In%20 the%20Mirror%20of%20the%20Past%20.pdf.
68 Quoted in Brett Milano, "To Understand Trump, Learn from His Voters," *Harvard Gazette*, 22 February 2017, https://news.harvard.edu/gazette/story/2017/02 /to-understand-trump-learn-from-his-voters/; Michael J. Sandel, *The Tyranny of Merit: What's Become of the Common Good?* (New York: Farrar, Straus and Giroux, 2020), chapters 1 and 4.
69 Illich, *Deschooling Society*, 10.

His critique and proposed alternative are based on the idea that people acquire most knowledge from outside the school, the school being by and large a place of confinement. He relates Paulo Freire's work with adult learners in Brazil who learned to read and write through the language of their own experience and goes into the idea of educational matching among people according to their needs and interests.[70]

At the beginning of the first chapter, Illich states that the institutionalization of values through schooling leads to a process of degradation and misery. He writes that "health, learning, dignity, independence, and creative endeavor are defined as little more than the performance of the institutions which claim to serve these ends and their improvement is made to depend on allocating more resources to the management of hospitals, schools, and other agencies in question."[71] At the core of his claim was a theological search for freedom, freedom of the will, and the self as agent, and a Thomistic concern with necessity as imposed; schooling had become an imposed necessity, yet natural necessity is not repugnant to the will.[72] Later in the book he wrote that the industrial technological society defines our needs.[73]

We can follow a thread in *Deschooling Society* and in other works that has to do with human beings recovering a sense of personal responsibility when teaching and learning, involving a transformation of consciousness in relation to the nature of learning that does not conceive learning as merchandise or as an institutional goal. Illich wrote: "By making men [*sic*] abdicate the responsibility for their own growth, school leads many to a kind of spiritual suicide."[74] Illich thought that to solve this it is necessary to launch a revolution against those forms of privilege and power that are an integral part of the right to have professional knowledge.

Illich asserted that the school system, instead of equalizing chances, has monopolized their distribution and that compulsory schooling polarizes society. He envisioned disestablished schools, which meant moving them away from the state. It is fascinating that in the first chapter of *Deschooling Society* Illich refers to Milton Friedman's system of tuition grants, through which funds would be channeled to the beneficiary, who in turn could buy a share of the schooling of her/his/their choice. Illich observed that if the credit was limited to purchases that

---

70   Illich, *Deschooling Society*, 18.
71   Illich, *Deschooling Society*, 1.
72   Thomas Aquinas, *Summa Theologica*, Part I, Question 82.
73   Illich, *Deschooling Society*, 36.
74   Illich, *Deschooling Society*, 60.

fit into a school curriculum, the tendency would be to provide greater equality of treatment, but this would not increase the equality of social claims.[75] At that time in the late 1960s, and certainly by the early 1970s, in the midst of dreams of revolution and social reform, the proposal had a reactionary tone. Friedman's proposals were actually implemented in Chile by General Pinochet after the coup d'état of 1973, along with a market approach and school privatization, the consequences of which we now know. It generated more inequality and another layer in the meritocratic system. In other words, Illich's proposal is quite separated from actual contexts and the agendas of the Chicago Boys and neoliberalism, which is what gives it an ahistorical character.

Illich also refers to Christopher Jencks of the Center for the Study of Public Policy, sponsored by the Office of Economic Opportunity, who proposed "to put educational 'entitlements' or tuition grants into the hands of parents and students for expenditure in the schools of their choice. Such individual entitlements could indeed be an important step in the right direction. We need a guarantee of the right of each citizen to an equal share of tax-derived educational resources."[76] Jencks's proposal, in Illich's view, condemns itself since the tuition grants would have to be spent on schooling. Illich was aware of the potential consequences of playing into the hands not only of professional educators, but, for example, racists and religious groups. It would discredit a central point, he said, namely, "the return of initiative and accountability for learning to the learner or his most immediate tutor."[77]

Sybil Shack, a distinguished, progressive-minded teacher from Winnipeg, Manitoba, Canada, responded to the presentations made at different times in Winnipeg in 1971 by Illich and Holt. While acknowledging that many of their biting criticisms could not be ignored, what was alarming for her was that they were advocating the destruction of the institution. (She had been politically militant in the quest for a just education and equal opportunities.) The alternatives they presented, particularly Illich, could lead, in Shack's words, "only to inequity at the best and chaos at the worst."[78] She was referring to the use of the voucher system: giving every parent a voucher and letting them select the school in which they thought their children would receive the best education. Illich's intentionality was not understood – he was looking

---

75   Illich, *Deschooling Society*, 6.

76   Illich, *Deschooling Society*, 16.

77   Illich, *Deschooling Society*, 16.

78   Sybil Shack, "Sybil Shack Says... It's Not Open Season on the Public School," *Monday Morning*, November 1971, 5–9, quotation on 5.

for an alternative outside of schooling, but the reader placed the alternative in the concrete context of the time and in line with Friedman's economic ideas. Shack wrote, "The voucher plan is receiving much publicity and favorable editorials. I can see its appeal. Here is private enterprise at its best. It sounds logical to let schools compete for excellence and for pupil enrolment. The poor schools would fall by the wayside."[79]

In the second chapter of *Deschooling Society*, "Phenomenology of School," Illich's critiques are certainly relevant, although he takes a nihilistic turn and neglects to consider negotiation, resistance, counterhegemonic views, and localization. Thus, the teacher is seen as a secular priest, "a man" [sic] who wears an invisible triple crown, like the papal tiara, the symbol of triple authority combined in one person," whom the child has to confront.[80] The teacher, he said, pontificates as pastor, prophet, and priest – a guiding teacher and administrator of sacred ritual. He wrote: "He [the teacher; sic] combines the claims of medieval popes in a society constituted under the guarantee that these claims shall never be exercised together by one established and obligatory institution – church or state."[81] He defines school "as the age-specific, teacher-related process requiring full-time attendance at an obligatory curriculum."[82] He saw the school as occupying the place the institutional church had occupied in the past and argued his point: "So the poor are robbed of their self-respect by subscribing to a creed that grants salvation only through the school. At least the church gave them a chance to repent at the hour of death. School leaves them with the expectation (a counterfeit hope) that their grandchildren will make it. That expectation is of course still more learning which comes from school but not from teachers." An interesting point is his questioning of the discovery and institutionalization of childhood: the notion that children belong in school.[83] Illich wrote: "Growing up through childhood means being condemned to a process of inhuman conflict between self-awareness and the role imposed by a society going through its own school age. Neither Stephen Daedalus [sic] nor Alexander Portnoy enjoyed childhood, and neither, I suspect, did many of us like to be treated as children."[84]

---

79 Shack, "Sybil Shack Says," 5.
80 Illich, *Deschooling Society*, 31.
81 Illich, *Deschooling Society*, 31.
82 Illich, *Deschooling Society*, 26.
83 Illich, *Deschooling Society*, 26.
84 Illich, *Deschooling Society*, 27.

In the chapter "Ritualization of Progress," Illich makes the case that educational institutions play the role common to powerful churches throughout history, as the "repository of society's myth, the institutionalization of that myth's contradictions, and the locus of the ritual which reproduces and veils the disparities between myth and reality."[85] He wrote, making his case and proposing a solution: "Today the school system, and specially the university, provides ample opportunity for criticism of the myth and for rebellion against its institutional perversions. But the ritual which demands tolerance of the fundamental contradictions between myth and institution still goes largely unchallenged, for neither ideological criticism nor social action can bring about a new society. Only disenchantment with and detachment from the central social ritual and reform of that ritual can bring about radical change."[86] Illich addressed knowledge distributed by schools as merchandise and education as a product of teaching to be consumed and for which one must attend school; this is what he called the myth of institutionalized values.[87] He also addressed the myth of measurement of values and denounced the criteria for evaluation used in schools and the curricula being broken into prefabricated blocks; what cannot be measured, in such an environment, becomes secondary. Illich referred to two more myths: the myth of packaging values – with packages of knowledge being sold by the school – and the myth of self-perpetuating progress – in reference to the permanent and growing process of consumption, with the consumer-pupils conforming their desires to marketable values.[88]

It is significant that Illich saw revolutionary potential in disestablishing schooling from the state in the same way as the church was disestablished all over the world during the last two centuries.[89] (We assume that he is referring to the Catholic Church in the Western world, mostly Europe). In June 1971, when his book was about to come out and around the same date he wrote the lines mentioned before, at the World Conference of Christian Education held in Lima, Peru, he said that he advocated the disestablishment of the school as an institution in

---

85 Illich, *Deschooling Society*, 37.
86 Illich, *Deschooling Society*, 37–8.
87 Illich, *Deschooling Society*, 47.
88 Illich, *Deschooling Society*, 38–47.
89 Ivan Illich, "The Alternative to Schooling," in *Alternatives in Education*, CIDOC *Cuaderno* vol. 1, no. 77 (Cuernavaca, Mexico: CIDOC, July 1971–June 1972), 324/1–9, see 324/1. First published in *Saturday Review*, New York, 19 June 1971, 44–8 and 59–60.

the same sense that the term "disestablishment" is used in the United States to talk about the separation of church and state.[90] The implication of his proposed solution is powerful. Deschooling, in his view, had the revolutionary potential to destroy the social order and was at the root of any movement of human liberation.[91]

In the chapter "Institutional Spectrum," Illich conceives schooling as the type of institution defined as manipulative, placing it on the right of the spectrum where he situates service institutions providing false utilities and the most influential modern institutions; on the left he places "convivial institutions," referring to institutions distinguished by their spontaneous use (public markets, subway lines, etc.). Other enterprises could be closer to the centre or to the left. He wrote: "Right-wing institutions tend to be highly complex and costly production processes in which much of the elaboration and expense is concerned with convincing consumers that they cannot live without the product or the treatment offered by the institution. Left-wing institutions tend to be networks which facilitate client-initiated communication or cooperation."[92]

His observation in the chapter called "Irrational Consistencies" regarding educational research is worth noting. He wrote: "An educational revolution depends on a twofold inversion: a new orientation for research and a new understanding of the educational style of an emerging counterculture."[93] A great deal of research in education today is geared towards covering the needs of the system.

The emerging technological revolution gave him grounds to find a way to replace the school. Illich foresaw educational webs as a possible alternative that would support learning in a deschooled milieu. Thus, in chapter 6, "Learning Webs," he makes the case that deschooling is possible. He puts forward the idea of self-motivated learning, rather than the need for a teacher to bribe or force the students to have the will to learn; the alternative would create new links to the world and would lead to responsible educational independence instead of funnelling educational programs through the teacher.[94] The overall general characteristics of the new formal educational institution should provide all who want to learn with access to available resources at any time

---

90 Ivan Illich, "La desescolarización de la iglesia [Deschooling the Church]," in Ivan Illich, *Obras Reunidas*, vol. 1 (Mexico: Fondo de Cultural Económica, 2008), 116–24.
91 Illich, *Deschooling Society*, 27.
92 Illich, *Deschooling Society*, 55.
93 Illich, *Deschooling Society*, 70.
94 Illich, *Deschooling Society*, 73.

in their lives; it should empower all who want to share what they know to match with those willing to learn that knowledge; and it should provide to those who want to present an issue to the public the opportunity to do so.[95] In moving ahead with the chapter on Learning Webs, his attack on the state is clear: "Even the piecemeal creation of new educational agencies which were the inverse of school would be an attack on the most sensitive link of a pervasive phenomenon, which is organized by the state in all countries. A political program which does not explicitly recognize the need for deschooling is not revolutionary."[96]

When discussing the learning webs and the need for deschooling, Illich said that the struggle against domination by the world market and big-power politics might be beyond poor communities' and countries' capabilities – a situation that added the reason, he added, for reversing their educational structure.[97] These statements give a glimpse into why he is today an inspiration to those engaged in alter-globalization and economic slowdown. At the time, one of the reviewers of Reimer's book, Wagschal, wrote that "ideas for opportunity networks, though interesting and imaginative, must be considered more cautiously than either he [Reimer] or Illich has done in their writing." Wagchal referred to the corporate interest in profiteering from this kind of educational de-institutionalization, and went as far as saying that in an era of claims for public control of health (health care) and law (juricare), "deschooling seems more like a reactionary proposal than a plea for viable radical reform."[98] Illich's critique is indeed radical, but his proposed alternative is not part of a socio-economic analysis; it reveals a lack of historical analysis and political ambiguity. Neither Illich nor Reimer, who maintained a similar thesis, saw the implications of their proposal.

Educational resources were labelled, Illich said, according to the goals of the curriculum. Instead, he labelled four different approaches that would enable students to gain access to any educational resource. These were: reference services to educational objects, skill exchanges, peer-matching – a communications network – and reference services through which educators at large could be listed in a directory. This system would require agreements that could be conceived as constitutional guaranties that would serve as a defence against the possibility of a compulsory curriculum or

---

95   Illich, *Deschooling Society*, 75.
96   Illich, *Deschooling Society*, 75.
97   Illich, *Deschooling Society*, 75.
98   H. Wagschal, "SCHOOL IS DEAD (Author: Everett Reimer)," *McGill Journal of Education / Revue Des Sciences De l'éducation De McGill* 7, no. 2 (1972), https://mje.mcgill.ca/article/view/6884.

demands for certification, and that would protect the taxpayer from paying for a gigantic apparatus of educators and their buildings.

Deschooling Society concludes with a chapter, "Rebirth of the Epimethean Man," that seems out of place, and it is one that was not part of the discussions with Everett Reimer.[99] The chapter deserves some attention because it provides a channel into Illich's conception of humanhood. In it, he goes back to the Prometheus myth of Greek mythology to question modern humanity, a conception that he worked on before the publication of *Deschooling Society* by Harper & Row. Here, Illich reinterprets the myth, writing that Hesiod's re-elaboration of the myth of Pandora, the All-Giver and Earth goddess, in what he describes as prehistoric matriarchal Greece, allows him to make a case for the replacement of hope with expectation. Hope means trusting faith in the goodness of nature, while expectation is planned and controlled by humans. The original Pandora, Illich writes, "was sent to Earth with a jar which contained all ills; of good things, it contained only hope."[100] She let all ills escape from her amphora, but closed the lid before Hope could escape.[101] In the classical form of the myth, Pandora releases both evils and goods and is remembered for the ills, and in the myth it was forgotten that the All-Giver is a keeper of hope. Epimetheus, a brother of Prometheus, which means "forethought," marries Pandora against his brother's will; the name Epimetheus, which means "hindsight," was given the meaning of dull or dumb. At the time, Illich continues, the Greeks had built a rational and authoritarian society led by misogynist patriarchs who "panicked at the thought of the first woman" and planned institutions to deal with the ills. Instead of interpreting dreams, the oracle was consulted on social and political options. The "classical man [*sic*] framed a civilized context for human perspective. He [Prometheus] was aware that he could defy fate-nature-environment, but only at his own risk."[102] Illich's language is metaphorical and poetic to some extent and grounded in the Catholic notion of hope (trust in providence and in a providential order). Illich is questioning here the notion of planning and places his narration at a time previous to classical Greece, characterized, following Illich, by an imaginary guided by hope. However, it has been interpreted as Illich referring to Jesus Christ through the figure of

---

99   For a sympathetic analysis of Illich, see José María Sbert, *Epimeteo, Iván Illich y el sendero de la sabiduría* (Mexico: n.p., 1996).

100   Illich, *Deschooling Society*, 106.

101   Illich, *Deschooling Society*, 105.

102   Illich, *Deschooling Society*, 107.

Figure 4.1. "Night of the Darwin Moon," by Angela Costello

Source: https://www.costello-prints.ca.
Silkscreen print on paper, 14" W x 33" H.

Epimetheus in an apophatic way (not mentioning God directly).[103] His primitive world, which he does not place historically, does not fit with the history of humanity. For example, when humans began to establish themselves as sedentary in a place 12,000 years ago, and to cultivate and domesticate animals and plants, they had to anticipate and plan; they also changed the way they related to the natural milieu, and there were changes in language and in mathematical thinking.[104]

Illich seems to talk of a world inspired by the Promethean ethos that he is relating to industrial modernity. This paragraph is illustrative:

> To the primitive the world was governed by fate, fact, and necessity. By stealing fire from the gods, Prometheus turned facts into problems, called necessity into question, and defied fate. Classical man [sic] framed a civilized context for human perspective. He [sic] was aware that he [sic] could defy fate-nature-environment, but only at his [sic] own risk. Contemporary man [sic] goes further; he [sic] attempts to create the world in his [sic] image, to build a totally man-made [sic] environment, and then discovers that he [sic] can do so only on the condition of constantly remaking himself [sic] to fit it. We now must face the fact that man himself [sic] is at stake.[105]

The original title of *Deschooling Society* was *The Dawn of Epimethean Man and Other Essays*. It was a suggestive title since, for Illich, humanity had lost the notion of hope with the dominance of the Promethean ethos that eclipsed hope and opened the way for a challenge of fate and to the notion of progress. Hope, faith, love were, in Illich's conception, traditional Catholic virtues replaced by expectation, planning, and charity, which represented the institutionalization of values.[106] It is as nostalgic as it is ahistorical. Contemporary humans built a totally human-made environment, and there is something structurally wrong with the vision of homo faber – from the destruction of the environment and the limits of earth's resources to consumerism and its deceptions. Illich wrote: "This institutionalization of substantive values, this belief that a planned process of treatment ultimately gives results desired by the recipient, this consumer ethos, is at the heart of the Promethean fallacy."[107]

---

103 Jorge Márquez Muñoz, "Prologo," in *Epimeteo, Iván Illich y el sendero de la sabiduría*, ed. José María Sbert (Mexico: Ediciones sin nombre, 2009), 11–25, particularly 9.

104 See Sue T. Parker and Constance Milbrath, "Higher Intelligence, Propositional Language, and Culture as Adaptations of Planning," in *Tools, Language and Cognition in Human Evolution*, ed. Kathleen R. Gibson and Tim Ingold (Cambridge: Cambridge University Press, 1993), 314–33.

105 Illich, *Deschooling Society*, 107.

106 See Colin Miller, "Ivan Illich, Catholic Theologian (Part I)," *Pro Ecclesia: A Journal of Catholic and Evangelical Theology* 26, no. 1 (2017): 81–110, see 83.

107 Illich, *Deschooling Society*, 114.

5 Going Back to *Deschooling Society*

Reflections after One More Reading of *Deschooling Society*

The key issues in *Deschooling Society* were the critique of the nation-state and its monopoly of education through schooling and its hidden curriculum (which in Illich's view defined a new class structure), the need for the rescue of the self as agent, the denunciation of the confusion of education with schooling – as was done before with the church and religion – and schooling as an imposed necessity. His solution to all of this was disestablishing schools, meaning moving them away from the state and searching for alternatives that do not conceive learning as merchandise or as an institutional goal.

The book condemns the school system and rejects any attempt at reforming the school as an institution. It is a radical position that is also the key argument in Everett Reimer's *School Is Dead*. The two books see schooling as being at the centre of the need for a drastic paradigmatic change in education and society, but they remain somewhat disconnected from the socio-economic context and potential alternative practices.[1]

Upon reading *Deschooling Society* again, we found that Illich's theological background – which, as Charles Taylor wrote, was both orthodox and iconoclastic[2] – and his Thomism led him to take a universalist

---

1 Some authors relying on statements and writings by Illich after *Deschooling Society* have stated that Illich did not suggest the complete elimination of schooling and that they consider this as a misinterpretation. For example, see Patricia Inman, *An Intellectual Biography of Ivan Illich* (PhD diss., Northern Illinois University, 1999). However, we are here to discuss *Deschooling Society*, not the overall viewpoint on schooling developed by Illich over time, although we discuss his own critique of *Deschooling Society* at the end of the chapter.

2 Charles Taylor, *A Secular Age* (Cambridge, MA: The Belknap Press of Harvard University Press, 2007), 737.

approach. There is, then, an aloofness towards the women's movement – a positioning that could be explained to some extent when reading his *Gender* (1982)[3] – and even towards the civil rights movement. There is little historical context in *Deschooling Society*, but there is a great deal of general exhortation.

It is noticeable how, in his emphasis on the parallelism of schools monopolizing education and the church dominating spiritual life in the Western world in previous centuries, Illich neglected to consider that schools and educational institutions have their own social, cultural, political, and economic contexts. He was looking for a free encounter for those who are learning, in the same way that he had wanted to liberate the message of God from the modernity that had led to the institutionalization of this message in the first place. However, he did not elaborate on a conception of education or of educational aims at various levels of human experience, and thus he reduced education to schooling, even as he seemed to differentiate between the two. There is no reference in the book to the role of the family, peers, or various social instances, including involvement in religious practices. Illich makes the case that systematic and continuing education might ensure an ever-growing demand and consumption for its products.[4] This may be so, but Illich bestowed on schooling tremendous power without hope or space for the exercise of agency.

There is another point we wish to make. As Bruno-Jofré wrote when discussing educationalization, "while it is important to recognize that subjects are conditioned by social, cultural, linguistic, political, and ideological forces, there is danger in embracing the idea of an individual or collective self as exhausted by those external forces."[5] In this case, the self is suffocated by schooling. Illich neither acknowledges "transgressions" in the life of schooling[6] nor all efforts at educational change, including experimentation in self-determination, progressive education, free schooling, critical education moving the educational process into the hands of the students, and the development of a critical consciousness through those pedagogical efforts. He rejects all education that can be understood as a systematic transfer of knowledge in favour

---

3   Ivan Illich, *Gender* (New York: Pantheon Books, 1982).

4   Illich, *Deschooling Society*, 27.

5   Rosa Bruno-Jofré, "Problematizing 'Educationalization,'" in *Educationalization and Its Complexities: Religion, Politics, and Technology*, ed. Rosa Bruno-Jofré (Toronto: University of Toronto Press, 2019), 3–26, quotation on 7.

6   Pierre Dominicé and Rosika Darcy de Oliveira, *Freire, Illich, the Pedagogy of the Oppressed, the Oppression of Pedagogy*, IDAC Document #8 (Geneva, 1974).

of an education that is spontaneous – one that has lost its institutional baggage and its scientific specialization.[7]

Perhaps the most poignant absence is in reference to the development of a body of scholarship on theories of learning, educational theory, psychology, the development of cognitive psychology, theories of child development, and ancillary sciences that brought knowledge that was incorporated into educative practices in schooling. A spontaneous education could not incorporate such knowledge or the claims of subaltern groups in society and the integration of their vindications. This is not part of his point, indeed, since Illich places himself outside the discourse of the public education that he critiques.

The critique Illich elaborates is sound in its highlighting of the social reproductive character of schooling, the links to the economy, the political agenda and the formation of a self-governed/self-regulated subject, and the limits of school meritocracy. However, the alternatives he proposes in *Deschooling Society* are not placed in the socio-economic context, and we can see now how a great deal of these alternatives have been incorporated into the system. For example, one of the largest businesses is teaching online with a new sense of the commons, albeit a disembodied one. Nonetheless, Illich's critique and alternatives may be construed as a vision enriched by his later work that will continue to inspire people searching for a common good.

Deschooling Society actually has an intuitive and visionary quality. As we have mentioned, Illich's understanding of the role of schooling in creating a class structure has become significant in explaining the emergence of populist governments, such as Trump's government and its accompanying Trumpism.[8] Post-modernists and anarchists have been attracted to *Deschooling Society*, and the reasons are apparent, in particular Illich's questioning of the state. Illich's eclectic positioning and argumentation were nourished by complex tendencies inside the Catholic Church, such as the questioning of modernity, and by his critique of the church as institution. The neo-Thomistic framework, a dualist theology – along with the residual neo-medievalist and anti-state elements in his thought – the influence of Maritain, and Illich's own experience in Cuernavaca and with CIDOC, as well as his exposure to psychoanalysis, anti-imperialist views, and Latin America moulded the intentionality behind his thinking at that point in his trajectory. Some of Illich's

---

7 Dominicé and de Oliveira, *Freire, Illich*, 16.
8 For example, see the thesis of Michael Sandel in *The Tyranny of Merit: What's Become of the Common Good?* (New York: Farrar, Straus and Giroux, 2020).

ideas in *Deschooling Society* are taken up in current futuristic visions of deschooling and relate to Illich's notion of conviviality.[9]

Deschooling Society embodies a phase in the personal and intellectual trajectory of Ivan Illich. It has to be read also in relation to his relationship to Everett Reimer, Paul Goodman, and other critics of education, and within the framework of the dramatic turn Illich took in 1967/8 from a critique of the institutional church to a critique of schooling, which marked the beginning of his analysis of secular institutions.

The relationship with Reimer is particularly important since they were both engaged in joint research on the same topic and in the end decided to go their separate ways, Illich with *Deschooling Society* and Reimer with *School Is Dead*. Reimer states that his book is the result of a conversation with Ivan Illich that lasted for fifteen years.[10] There is a statement in Illich's book saying that they had decided to publish separate views.[11] There are similitudes in terms of the argument against compulsory schooling, and, as Reimer puts it, around contradictions in the world that could be corrected by freeing education from the school so that people can learn about their society. Reimer considers educational networks as a way to free people from compulsory schooling, involving funds that would go from public schooling to the student in the form of credits. He starts by saying that "school has become the universal church of a technological society, incorporating and transmitting its ideology, shaping men's [*sic*] minds to accept this ideology, and conferring social status in proportion to its acceptance."[12] Reimer wrote: "No child, however, fails to learn from school. Those who never get in learn that the good things of life are not for them. Those who drop out early learn that they do not deserve the good things of life. The later dropouts learn that the system can be beaten, but not by them. All of them learn that school is the path to secular salvation, and resolve that their children shall climb further on the ladder than they did."[13] Illich wrote in *Deschooling Society*, "Equal educational opportunity is, indeed, both a desirable and a feasible goal, but to equate this with obligatory schooling is to confuse salvation with the church. School has become

---

9 Petar Jandrić, "Deschooling Virtuality," *Open Review of Educational Research* 1 (2014): 84–98, https://www.tandfonline.com/doi/full/10.1080/23265507.2014.965193 ?scroll=top&needAccess=true#.

10 Everett Reimer, *School Is Dead: An Essay on Alternatives in Education* (New York: Penguin Education Specials, Kindle version; originally published by Penguin, 1971), location 15.

11 Illich, *Deschooling Society*, xx.

12 Reimer, *School Is Dead*, location 2.

13 Reimer, *School Is Dead*, location 116.

the world religion of a modernized proletariat, and makes futile promises of salvation to the poor of the technological age."[14]

While Illich compiled somewhat disconnected papers (he called them pamphlets) for the book, Reimer from the beginning aimed at publishing a book with its own chapters in logical sequence. Both authors make extreme generalizations. Wagschal, in his review of Reimer's book, said that there was no attempt to distinguish between countries; whether the school was in Mexico or Europe, it was, for Reimer, an institution preventing individuals from having a degree of self-realization.[15] The point here is that both books were the product of a lengthy conversation between the two men, although Illich nurtured his positioning with theological ideas. They have to be read in the context of the time, too, including the impact of Michael Young's *The Rise of the Meritocracy*, and the work of Paul Goodman, Kozol, and others.

Illich had engaged in a severe critique of the church as It, as a corrupt oppressive institution, while under Spellman's protection. But when he lost his protection upon Spellman's death in December 1967 and when the Vatican tried to condemn him in 1968, he was able to halt the condemnation and continue on with his activities and independence. He left aside the critique of the church and moved to a critique of schooling, and he would later go on to a critique of modern institutions in various phases of his intellectual life. *Deschooling Society* was inspired by a critique of the church as It within the context of a critique of modernity – a critique that came from Illich's profound and direct knowledge of the corruption and hypocrisy of the church (Illich having studied and worked in the Vatican before going to New York). Illich's silence on Spellman, an example of the corruption of the church as It, is deafening.

Illich's original contribution in this book resides in his critique of schooling within the context of modernity, and in his ideas around a recovery of teaching and learning as a personal responsibility at the core of human experience – and beyond institutions. An important point that is often missed is that his understanding of free learning was integral to his search for the freedom in God. However, he did not see, in *Deschooling Society*, the school as he saw the church as She (the tradition, the spirituality to be kept). Notably, while Illich was critical of educational institutions and their expansion in industrial societies, and of the perversion of the free relations of people and their mediating role, he was himself a product of the best recognized high school and

---

14 Illich, *Deschooling Society*, 10.
15 Wagschal, "SCHOOL IS DEAD."

universities in the world: from the Institute of Florence, to the Pontifical Gregorian University, to the University of Salzburg.

As discussed earlier, Illich had planned in 1973 that he would close CIDOC in 1976, thirteen years after its creation. It was closed, too, at the right time, something you can expect from a visionary. In the first quarter of the 1970s, there was a recession of radical politics worldwide. The apocalyptic visions of the early 1970s eased with the US economic recovery after the stagnation of 1973–5 in most of the Western world. In the United States, the new Christian right, moral conservatives, blue-collar Reaganites, the nascent green movement, and consumerists emerged as important forces, with bloc and interest group voting being the rule.[16]

The Cold War welfare state ended with the economic and political shifts of the 1970s and 1980s and the beginning era of finance capitalism that ushered in neoliberalism; the global economy would take new shape, entering into what we know as late capitalism. Dictatorships were established in many Latin American countries in the 1970s; in 1979, the year of the revolution in Nicaragua, the guerrilla war against the governing military junta started in El Salvador, which would entail US intervention against the leftist organizations. The political context changed dramatically from the early years of the 1970s.

The end of CIDOC had repercussions for Illich's intellectual life. The centre was an international hub for the critical analysis of modern institutions by avant-garde intellectuals, politicians, and leaders of the countercultural movement from around the world. The times had changed. CIDOC was the point of contact with the Latin American political reality, and unlike Paulo Freire, Sergio Méndez Arceo, Augusto Salazar Bondy, and others – who had some connection with CIDOC – Illich did not position himself in line with the grassroots political movements in Latin America, or with movements resisting oppression. CIDOC had been the space within and through which he had maintained his commitment to social and political change in Latin America. He would enter into a new rich path in his intellectual life.

Illich's Early "Recanting" of Deschooling Society[17]

Illich, in retrospect, in his 1995 Foreword to Deschooling Our Lives, edited by Matt Hern, referred to "The Alternative to Schooling," the

---

16 Daniel T. Rodgers, *Age of Fracture* (Cambridge, MA: The Belknap Press of Harvard University Press, 2011), 79 and 80.

17 We acknowledge that large components of this part to the end of the chapter come, with permission, from our article, "Ivan Illich's Late Critique of *Deschooling Society*:

article in *Saturday Review* that was published during the week *Deschooling Society* came out, as his own recantation.[18] He wrote in the article that he had argued, "the alternative to schooling was not some other type of educational agency, or the design of educational opportunities in every aspect of life, but a society which fosters a different attitude of people toward tools."[19] (We know that institutions are tools in his framework.) Illich's interpretation was not very clear in the text of "The Alternative to Schooling," although the closing lines could be construed as a hint in relation to his own reconstruction of his positioning expounded in *Deschooling Society*. He concluded that deschooling the culture and social structure would require the use of technology to generate participatory politics; he advocated a new environment in which growing up classless would be possible. Illich did not want Big Brother to educate all of us.[20] The interpretative move he describes in the "Foreword" written in 1995 does not appear in the exchange with Freire in 1975.

The exchange with Paulo Freire in Geneva in 1975, five years after the publication of both Freire's *Pedagogy of the Oppressed* and the first version (entitled *The Dawn of Epimethean Man and Other Essays*) of what would be *Deschooling Society* published by Harper & Row in 1971, is illustrative. Freire pointed out that Illich erred in refusing to analyse the ideological question, and for that reason he was unable to understand the phenomenon in its entirety.[21] Illich was not prepared to discuss the matter at that time. Freire had concerns about Illich's understanding of the school as an institution that possessed a demonic essence that had either to be suppressed or surpassed, without looking at the issues from an ideological perspective. Freire, in contrast, believed that the ideological force behind schooling as a social institution could be changed and that reform efforts should work towards such ideological change.[22] Their starting point was quite different. Freire was inspired by a social

---

'I Was Largely Barking Up the Wrong Tree,'" *Educational Theory* 62, no. 5 (2012): 573–92. We have reproduced here paragraphs from pages 586 to 592, with minor modifications.

18 Ivan Illich, "The Alternative to Schooling." Originally published in *Saturday Review*, New York, 19 June 1971, 44–8 and 59–60.

19 Ivan Illich, "Foreword," in *Deschooling Our Lives*, ed. Matt Hern (Philadelphia: New Society Publishers, 1996), vii–x, quotation on viii.

20 Illich, "The Alternative to Schooling."

21 Paulo Freire and Ivan Illich, *La educación: Autocrítica [Education: Self-Criticism]* (Buenos Aires: Ediciones Búsqueda, 1986).

22 Paulo Freire, "La dimensión política de la educación: [The Political Dimension of Education]," *Cuadernos Pedagógicos*, no. 8 (Quito, Ecuador: CEDECO, 1985); Carlos Alberto Torres, *Paulo Freire en América Latina: Materiales para una crítica de la pedagogia*

reading of the gospel, his own pedagogical practice with the oppressed, and the development of liberation theology. Illich was a Thomist and saw the church as a spiritual force in society.

In "The Alternative to Schooling," Illich addressed reform in line with the idea that education had become the search for "an alchemic process that would bring forth a new type of man [sic], who would fit into an environment created by scientific magic."[23] He classified those reformers who realized the system was failing into three groups: a) the great masters of alchemy who promised better schools; b) the popular magicians who wanted to make every kitchen into an alchemic lab; c) and the Masons of the Universe, who wanted to transform the world into a temple of learning. The masters of alchemy included a number of research directors employed or sponsored by foundations who believed schools could be economically feasible, and those concerned with curriculum and the packaging of new courses "on African culture, North American Imperialism, Women's Lib, Pollution" to allow students to decide what they would be taught.[24] The comment is alarming because he left aside the struggles of the 1960s to insist again that schools were prison houses. He was aware that some changes produced good effects, but they were, in his view, within narrow limits.[25] Illich was critical, too, of free schools because in order to be truly free, they had to prevent the hidden curriculum of graded attendance – a ritual of initiation into modern society – and provide a framework that would allow all participants to free themselves from the hidden foundations of a schooled society – these are fundamental assumptions about growing up, such as the relevance of being a "certified consumer of knowledge."[26] Illich wanted an education that would not be used to establish or justify a particular system or become the reason to measure a student following an abstract structure in order to suppress, control, or diminish. He wrote in the article on which we are commenting, "The scientific measurement of each man's [sic] 'educability to this full humanity' would finally coincide. Under the appearance of a 'free' market, the global village would turn into an environmental womb where pedagogic therapists control the complex navel by which each man [sic] is nourished."[27] He later saw this apocalyptic vision of global education as an early

problematizadora de Paulo Freire [Paulo Freire in Latin America: Materials for a Critical Pedagogy of Paulo Freire's Problematizing Pedagogy] (Mexico: Ediciones Gernika, 1979).

23 Illich, "The Alternative to Schooling," 324/3.
24 Illich, "The Alternative to Schooling," 324/3.
25 Illich, "The Alternative to Schooling," 324/3.
26 Illich, "The Alternative to Schooling," 324/4.
27 Illich, "The Alternative to Schooling," 324/5.

shift in his understanding of education, one that would inspire efforts at alter-globalization and of supranational organizations.

Illich's Own Critique of Deschooling: "I Was Largely Barking Up the Wrong Tree"

In 1995 Illich wrote the following in the Foreword to *Deschooling Our Lives*, mentioned above: "While my criticism of schooling in that book [*Deschooling Society*] may have helped some people reflect on the unwanted social side effects of that institution – and perhaps pursue meaningful alternatives to it – I now realize that I was largely barking up the wrong tree."[28] He said that at the time he wrote *Deschooling Society*, "I still accepted that, fundamentally, educational needs of some kind were an historical given of human nature. I no longer accept this today."[29] Let's trace his thinking.

After a hiatus of many years, Illich went back to his early work on education. During this period of his intellectual life, education was one of the certainties that Illich critiqued as being the result of tools (institutions) shaping our view of reality. In 1986 he wrote,

> To make my plea for this novel research plausible, I will explain the steps which led me to my present position. This I will do by criticizing my own *Deschooling Society* for its naïve views. My travelogue begins sixteen years ago, at a point when that book was about to appear. During the nine months the manuscript was at the publishers, I grew more and more dissatisfied with its texts. This misapprehension I owe to Cass Canfield, Harper's owner, who named my baby, and, in doing so, misrepresented my thoughts. … Since then my curiosity and reflections have focused on the historical circumstances under which the very idea of educational needs can arise.[30]

In the Foreword of 1995, Illich pointed to three moments in his intellectual journey, starting with the publication of *Deschooling Society*. The first moment, with his understanding of education as the point of reference, included the texts that would become *Deschooling Society* in 1971. About this first moment, Illich wrote, "I called for the disestablishment of schools for the sake of improving education and here, I noticed,

---

28 Illich, "Foreword," in *Deschooling Our Lives*, vii.
29 Illich, "Foreword," in *Deschooling Our Lives*, ix.
30 Ivan Illich, "A Plea for Research on Lay Literacy," *North American Review* 272, no. 3 (1987): 10–17, quotation on 11.

made my mistake. Much more important than the disestablishment of schools, I began to see, was the reversal of those trends that make of education a pressing need rather than a gift of gratuitous leisure."[31]

The second moment in Illich's intellectual journey occurred in the five years following the publication of *Deschooling Society*, when he realized that even liberating education from the state's monopoly would not be enough because the state and the modern industrial society had a variety of "educational" tools designed to put people's views into conformance with dominant ideology. The texts Illich wrote just after *Deschooling Society* was published were to an extent a response to the criticism of that book. In a paper he presented at the 1971 Christian Education World Assembly in Lima, Peru, entitled "La desescolarización de la iglesia" (Deschooling the Church), Illich stressed how the fundamental aspects of modern society had been inculcated through schooling (for example, by means of methods of instruction accumulating canned life), while also denouncing the pseudoreligious character of "education."[32] He prepared the terrain for understanding education as one of the certainties of modernity. In this sense, his critique in *Deschooling Society* would not mean much without differentiating education from learning – the latter being planned, measurable, and imposed on another person. About this second moment Illich pointed out,

> Largely through the help of my friend and colleague Wolfgang Sachs, I came to see that the educational function was already emigrating from the schools and that, increasingly, other forms of compulsory learning would be instituted in modern society. It would become compulsory not by law, but by other tricks such as making people to pay huge amounts of money in order to be taught how to have better sex, how to be more sensitive, how to know more about the vitamins they need, how to play games, and so on. This talk of "lifelong learning" and "learning needs" has thoroughly polluted society, and not just schools, with the stench on education.[33]

In the third moment of his intellectual journey during the 1980s and 1990s, Illich questioned the discourse behind the notion of educational needs, learning needs, and preparation for life (that is, lifelong learning). This third moment, neglected by historians, is of interest here. In fact, Illich realized then that when he wrote *Deschooling Society*, the

---

31 Illich, "Foreword," in *Deschooling Our Lives*, viii.
32 Ivan Illich, "La desescolarización de la iglesia [Deschooling the Church]," in Ivan Illich, *Obras Reunidas*, vol. 1 (Mexico: Fondo de Cultura Económica, 2006), 116–24.
33 Illich, "Foreword," in *Deschooling Our Lives*, viii.

social effects rather than the historical substance of education were at the core of his interest. Illich reflected that, in the past, he had called into question schooling as a desirable means, but not as a desirable end. As he wrote in 1995, "I still accepted that, fundamentally, educational needs of some kind were an historical given of human nature. I no longer accept this today."[34] In addition, during this third moment, Illich critiqued educational institutions without a particular aim beyond critique, providing no alternative and even rejecting the alternatives he had proposed in *Deschooling Society*. It is a creative critique without an ulterior response and with an ahistorical touch, which makes his later readings hard to analyse, particularly in relation to schooling. It is difficult to use Illich's critique as a transformative tool. Furthermore, his understanding should be read again in the context of his understanding of learning as a search for freedom in God and his reading of the parable of the Good Samaritan, which we will analyse below.

As he shifted his focus from schooling to education, from the process to its orientation, Illich reflected in the 1980s, "I came to understand education as 'acquired knowledge' under conditions that postulate scarcity of the means to acquire it."[35] In fact, his understanding that humans naturally belonged to the species *homo educandus* weakened when he studied economic conceptions and, in particular, when he read Karl Polanyi. From this perspective, the need for education as planned learning, which Illich seemed to equate with instruction and transmission of knowledge, was the result of ideas and arrangements that make the means for insertion in the school web scarce. The "educational rituals" reinforced faith in the value of knowledge acquired under conditions of scarcity. Illich further questioned the construction of ideals that could be educational aims and the pursuit of the ideal of the educated person.

The parable of the Good Samaritan is central to Illich's thinking. In the parable Illich finds an example to illustrate how human relations have changed since God's message was revealed. His central point is that while Jesus tried to respond to the question "Who is my neighbour?" modern thought interpreted the parable as referring to how one should behave towards one's neighbour.[36] We can transfer this to education in the sense that it implies a duty and breaks with God's message that gives us the freedom to choose the fellow humans with

---

34 Illich, "Foreword," in *Deschooling Our Lives*, ix.
35 Illich, "A Plea for Research," 12.
36 David Cayley, *The Rivers North of the Future: The Testament of Ivan Illich as Told to David Cayley* (Toronto: House of Anansi Press, 2005), 50–1.

whom we wish to associate beyond artificial constraints, such as the creation of a particular community – in other words, my neighbour is who I choose, not who I must choose. In Illich's interpretation, there is no way of categorizing who my neighbour ought to be. He believed that such an interpretation is the opposite of what Jesus wanted to point out. He had not asked how one should behave towards one's neighbour but, rather, "Who is my neighbour?": "Perhaps the only way we could recapture it today could be to imagine the Samaritan as a Palestinian ministering to a wounded Jew. He is someone who not only goes outside his ethnic preference for taking care of his own kind but who commits a kind of treason by caring for his enemy. In so doing he exercises a freedom of choice whose radical novelty has often been overlooked."[37] This story represents the possibility of breaking with ethical boundaries and exercising freedom of choice, having God as referent.[38]

This led to Illich's revised thinking about education, since freedom of choice became more and more institutionalized and reached its zenith with compulsory schooling – the obligation to be in touch with others instead of exercising free choice in the selection. As a result, Illich claimed that the schools would exemplify a perversion of the parable and its Christian message:

> In earlier talks I tried to make it plausible that the Christian message explosively expands the scope of love by inviting us to love whomever we choose. There is a new freedom involved, and a new confidence in one's freedom. I also tried to establish that this new freedom makes a new type of betrayal possible. The way I was led to frame this hypothesis was by observing the modern mania for education and then concluding that the only way it can be explained is as the fruit of a 2,000-year institutionalization of the catechetical, or instructional, function of the Christian

---

37 Cayley, *The Rivers North of the Future*, 50–1.
38 Within the context of the history of proportionality, Illich said that "nothing can exist without being dysymmetrically proportional to something else and that this dysymmetric proportionality is the reason for the existence of both." He went on to say, "'I' precisely because of you, by allowing me to love you, give me the possibility to be co-relative to you, to be dysymmetrically proportionate to you. I see, therefore, in love, hope, and charity the crowning of the proportional nature of creation in the full, old sense of that term." See Cayley, *The Rivers North of the Future*, 197. This statement is in line with Catholic theology and has controversial implications, in particular with reference to gender. See Gloria Bowles, "Introduction: The Context," *Feminist Issues* 3, no. 1 (1983): 3–6; Arlie Hochschild, "Illich: The Ideologue in Scientist's Clothing," *Feminist Issues* 3, no. 1 (1983): 6–11.

community, which has led us to believe that only through explicit teaching and through rituals in which teaching has a major part can we become fit for the community in which we ought to live.[39]

Charles Taylor also refers to Illich's interpretation of the parable of the Good Samaritan to explain the "great disembedding" that opened doors to another kind of solidarity beyond sacred social boundaries. Taylor acknowledges that it was, in a sense, a "corruption" of the Gospel as expounded by Illich, since we did not get "a network of agape but rather a disciplined society in which categorical relations have primacy, and therefore norms."[40] Illich's radical negation of any ideal led him to argue that only God can inspire human action and, further, that in a direct relationship with each human being, one can find God in the other. He critiqued education from an apophatic perspective; education, as he understood it – as planned learning – is a barrier between the individual who wishes to learn and the other, having in mind that the other is God.

Therefore, Illich explicitly distinguished the history of education from the history of *homo educandus*. The history of education, he argued, assumed that education is inherent to human existence, a historical given. He rejected this idea along with its concomitant understanding that in every human culture there is a stock of knowledge that has to be transmitted from generation to generation.[41] On the other hand, he said, the history of *homo educandus* studied the steps through which education as a necessity (need) came into existence historically: "The history of *homo educandus* deals with the emergence of a social reality within which 'education' [planned learning] is perceived as a basic human need."[42] From this perspective, Illich wrote, the "need" for education appears as a result of societal beliefs and arrangements that make the means for so-called socialization scarce. He went on to say, "I began to notice that educational rituals reflected, reinforced, and actually created belief in the value of learning pursued under conditions of scarcity. Such beliefs, arrangements, and rituals, I came to see, could easily survive and thrive under the rubrics of deschooling, free schooling, or

---

39 Cayley, *The Rivers North of the Future*, 145.
40 Charles Taylor, *A Secular Age* (Cambridge, MA: The Belknap Press of Harvard University Press, 2007), 158.
41 Ivan Illich, "The History of *Homo Educandus*" (1984), in Ivan Illich, *In the Mirror of the Past: Lectures and Addresses, 1978–1990* (New York and London: Marion Boyars, 1992).
42 Illich, "The History of *Homo Educandus*," 113.

homeschooling (which, for the most part, are limited to the commendable rejection of authoritarian methods)."[43]

For Illich, as institutions developed, administered, and categorized the encounter among fellow humans and the learning process, the sense of scarcity became dominant. These institutions would thus be a consequence of the process of corruption of the gospel and of the notion of hospitality, as they remove Christian responsibility from the individual. As a result, Illich wrote the following about *Deschooling Society* in his later years: "If people are seriously to think about deschooling their life, and not just escape from the corrosive effects of compulsory schooling, they could do no better than to develop the habit of setting a mental question mark beside all discourse on young people's 'educational needs' or 'learning needs,' or about their need for a 'preparation for life.' I would like them to reflect on the historicity of these very ideas. Such reflection would take the new crop of deschoolers a step further from where the younger and somewhat naïve Ivan was situated, back when talk of 'deschooling' was born."[44]

We think in light of what we have said that *Deschooling Society* needs to be examined in light of Illich's early clarifications but also in relation to the three shifting moments that he himself identified as important in his intellectual journey. The first moment (and we focus on education) is embodied in *Deschooling Society*, an apophatic text in which he advocated the liberation of the school from the state and proposed possible alternatives. The second moment, which occurred during the years immediately following the publication of *Deschooling Society*, corresponds with Illich's denunciation of the pseudoreligious character of education and his increasing awareness of how the educational functions were migrating from schools. He started to move towards understanding education as one of the certainties of modernity during this period. His most significant epistemological and personal shift, however, occurred in the 1980s, opening up what he identified as the third moment in an emerging intellectual context in which he was an active interlocutor. At this point, he no longer accepted the notion of educational needs, and, inspired by Karl Polanyi, he developed an understanding of knowledge acquired under conditions of scarcity. His critique of educational institutions during this period did not have a particular aim beyond critique; he did not propose alternatives of any kind. His critique of education as one of the certainties of modernity

---

43 Illich, "Foreword," in *Deschooling Our Lives*, ix.
44 Illich, "Foreword," in *Deschooling Our Lives*, x.

was intertwined with his analysis of the parable of the Good Samaritan and his belief that modernity is an outcome of a corrupted Christianity.

In the last stage of his life, Illich did not seem to be willing to go beyond a critique of certainties into suggestions for practice. This is encapsulated in what he said to Cayley at the end of his recorded testimony: "I hope nobody takes what I said for answers." Furthermore, although postmodernist and poststructuralist pedagogues may consider Illich an appealing author, it is important to keep in mind that the objective of his critique of modernity was to "save" the message and the grace of God that had been perverted by modernity.[45]

---

45 Cayley, *The Rivers North of the Future*, 299.

Index